My Pointless Struggle

My Pointless Struggle
(Waruagaki)
© Yohei Kitazato 2020
First published in Japan in 2020 by North Village, Tokyo.
English translation rights arranged with North Village, Tokyo.

ISBN: 978-1-64273-113-2

Written by Yohei Kitazato
Translated by Eric Margolis
English Edition Published by One Peace Books 2021

Printed in Canada
1 2 3 4 5 6 7 8 9 10

One Peace Books
43-32 22nd Street STE 204 Long Island City New York 11101
www.onepeacebooks.com

My Pointless Struggle

Yohei Kitazato

When I was a child, my teachers told me countless times:
Do your homework. Don't get into fights. Don't cause anyone trouble. Take things seriously.

Get a good score on your tests. Get into a good college, because if you don't, your future will be ruined. Listen to what your teachers say. You're a bad student because you never listen.

Be a diligent, hardworking child!

But when I finally finished school, through all of the studying and rules and preparations for adulthood, I found that my future was yet another command: find a job.

Hang on now, wait just a minute.
All of that, just to find a job? You're telling me that there's no other way to live my life?

It turned out that in all those years of schooling, I hadn't learned a single thing. Rather than choosing a job, wasn't it more important to choose how to live the rest of my life? Rather than learning how to get a perfect score, wouldn't it have been more useful for me to learn how to achieve my dreams?

What the hell? I felt I had been deceived.

I suppose all those adults just wanted to raise a kid that would make things easy for themselves. What a joke.

So, I decided to stop listening to what the so-called adults had told me.

Is it wrong to do what you love? Is it wrong to live the way you want to live?

"At some point, you need to just give up," they told me. "Listen to what we say. You have to start working at some point. You have to be realistic."

Excuse me? Who do they think they are—the adults that have already given up on every last one of their hopes and dreams—telling *me* what to do?

It's my life! I'll turn what I love doing for fun into what I do for a living. I'll continue to work towards the life that I dream about.

I decided to give up giving up. I decided to keep pushing closer to my dreams, to keep fighting my pointless struggle.

I decided to be free today, tomorrow, and every day until I die.

This is the story of my adventure.

Prologue
REUNION...10

Chapter One
MEETING KING...15

Chapter Two
A BOUT OF STRENGTH..33

Chapter Three
THE ANYWHERE DOOR...46

Chapter Four
A LEGENDARY JOURNEY..68

Chapter Five
FLIP THE SWITCH...93

Chapter Six
HYPER-FOCUS: MY OWN WORLD...116

Chapter Seven
SO, WHAT AM I?...124

Chapter Eight
THE STREETS TEACH YOU BOTH PLEASURE AND PAIN.......135

Chapter Nine
WANDERING..143

Chapter Ten
IF COMPANIES CHANGE, SO WILL THE WORLD......................147

Chapter Eleven
TO BE ONE OF THE PEOPLE WHO CAN PUBLISH A BOOK......173

Chapter Twelve
A PROMISE IS A PROMISE..219

Chapter Thirteen
GOODBYE, KING..228

Epilogue
NORTH VILLAGE...249

Prologue
REUNION

I had a few seconds left.

In a few seconds, the bell would ring.

The fight was about to start. I had to get ready. But my body and mind were held captive by a sensation I'd never felt before, and I couldn't move.

What was this strange feeling?

When you're in the fighting ring, you have no allies. I knew that my friends were sitting out there in the stands. I knew they were there, but I couldn't hear their voices.

It was very quiet.

It was as if all sounds—no, everything—had vanished from the world. The only thing I could see was my own hands. Both of my hands were wrapped in unfamiliar boxing gloves. I only noticed the color—black—and they felt so heavy that I could hardly move them. I wasn't even able to lift my head to see who I was facing.

Across from me, in the ring's opposite corner, stood the nine-time lineal super flyweight boxing champion. Masamori Tokuyama.

I could feel his bloodlust from across the ring, rising like a wave. When the bell rang, they were going to let the starved lion out of his cage. That bell was going to tell me that it was time to fight a lion barehanded.

There's no way you can do it. You'll be killed.

My body was immobile, petrified. Cold sweat crawled down my back. The solitary word *regret* floated to mind. *Why am I even standing here?*

I was twenty-five years old, an average employee in the finance department at Hitachi, Ltd. And I had never boxed before.

A few seconds had passed. It was time.

In those few seconds that felt like an eternity, finally, I understood. *So this is what true fear is like, huh?*

Of course, I had been afraid before. But the fear that I could feel now was something different entirely. My legs were locked in place, unable to even tremble. Cold sweat poured over my body in buckets and I couldn't even raise my voice or my eyes to meet my opponent's. This was the first time in my life I had ever experienced mortal fear.

A few months earlier, I was a spectator at a boxing match in the holy temple of martial arts, Korakuen Hall. It was the first time I had seen boxing, and the sheer intensity, the fervor of the ring, fascinated me. After the match, as the excitement faded, I went to the bathroom. I did my business, and as I was washing my hands, I looked at the mirror and all of the sudden fell back into a childhood memory.

When I was in kindergarten, I had yearned to be one of the strong heroes from *CoroCoro Comic* and *Shonen Jump* manga.

Those heroes did as they pleased and never gave up in their fights. I spent my childhood imitating those characters. I had full confidence that as an adult, I'd be able to stand shoulder to shoulder with those heroes.

But when I looked at myself in the mirror as a twenty-five-year-old, I realized that the version of myself that I had believed in didn't exist at all.

After all, up until now I had never fought in a real fight like in the ring—a real fight like this one. Even if I did whatever I wanted outside of the boxing ring, I had never risen to a true challenge, a true fight.

I was like a bystander. An outfielder. But I wanted to be the pitcher. I wanted to be important. I saw the person I was—a person who had let go of his childhood dream—and I was pathetic.

On the way home, the image of my face in the mirror and the boxers in the ring circled in my thoughts.

I had already decided to live my life just for the fun of it, but I started to wonder if that was the same thing as running away from the sight of a challenge. I realized that I had forgotten the feeling of really wanting to make a dream come true—no matter how hard, or painful.

That night, I couldn't bear it anymore. I wrote down my thoughts in an official letter of challenge to Masamori Tokuyama, who reigned at the top of the boxing world.

That's why I was standing there in the ring.

When I climbed up into the ring to face off against Tokuyama, I knew that I still couldn't say that I achieved my childhood dream of wanting to become a powerful hero. I couldn't say that I even deserved to stand in the same ring as a boxing champion. But still, I did it. I did it for myself.

This was a stage for settling my own dreams and aspirations.

When I realized it all, in that moment of darkness, silence, and stillness, I heard a familiar voice.

"It's been a while."

Even without turning around, I knew who that voice belonged to, and it wasn't one of my friends in the crowd. It was someone who I had known since fourth grade, who called himself King.

I could tell it was him by his husky voice. He was unshaven, wore old, ragged clothes, and had a strong build. He always had a sly smile—a twinkle in his eyes. King was standing behind me.

I had a lot I wanted to tell him. But I swallowed my words. I didn't have time to look behind me—the moment that I realized he was there, flashing lights and a roar that sounded like fireworks going off told me I had to face what was in front of me.

My body wasn't frozen anymore. The cold sweat on my back had disappeared.

I raised my head.

The champion, whom I had been too terrified to even make eye contact with, was standing in front of me. He stared at me intently, but for a moment, I saw a friendly smile cross his face, as if to say: *Good work. You made it to the ring.*

And then the bell rang out, telling me to move my life forward.

Chapter One
MEETING KING

It had been a long-time dream of mine to stand on that stage and hear that bell.

I'll say it at the risk of judgment—I grew up with a silver spoon, in a happy, well-to-do family. My parents were kind, sometimes strict—they weren't so lenient as to buy me whatever I wanted. But still, they could provide me with the things I needed, and fortunately for me, manga fit into the category of necessities.

Back in elementary school, I wasn't exactly in love with literature. My favorite "book" was *CoroCoro Comic*, a monthly comic magazine. Even though pretty much the only thing I ever read was comics, I still got perfect grades in school, including in Japanese studies.

Again, at the risk of judgment, I was basically a genius. At the least, that's what I thought about myself.

"When you were born, your father and I gave you plenty of talent to work with," my mom would tell me. "If at any point in your life you think 'I can't do it' or 'I can't win,' it won't be because of lack of talent—it will be because of lack of effort." Whenever I heard her tell me I had plenty of talent, it became another piece of evidence for me that I was a genius.

My mother was always kind to me. Besides from referring

to her own age as "a forever twenty-something," I never heard her tell a lie. I never heard her talk behind other people's backs, nor did I see any dark side of her whatsoever. So when my mother told me that line, without reservation, when I was an elementary schoolboy, I accepted it at face value.

In some ways, that's the case even today. I still believe that I'm a genius—in fact, I've never doubted it in my life. And to my parents who raised me that way, I say thank you!

Whenever I tell people that I'm a genius, they tend to laugh and say, "Well, that's silly." There are also friendly people who worry and fret about me for thinking that way. I always respond with a serious expression.

"I'm even more of a genius for thinking that I'm a genius," I tell them.

Usually they don't have a response to that. They must be thinking, "This guy has totally lost it, so whatever I say won't even make a difference."

Most people are far too humble and always make excuses for themselves, so of course they don't understand. But because I know that I'm a genius, I can chase after any dream under the sun.

But even a baseless, self-declared kid-genius like myself had problems. In fact, I had problems exactly *because* I was such a genius.

I thought about all of the soldiers in my beloved *CoroCoro*

Comic or on TV. Among them, there were a few heroes—strong, straightforward, and able to take down any challenge. For me, who really longed to become one of those heroes, my problem was simple:

Just what exactly am I?

I thought about it very seriously. On the one hand, I was just an elementary school kid, running around with snot hanging out of my nose until I collapsed from exhaustion. When I came home, I dove into TV and manga. I enjoyed my mom's delicious cooking, and after dinner, while my dad and sister happily talked, I went back to my room to do my homework. I was completely satisfied! That was enough to send me into blissful sleep.

You may be thinking: "That's just a normal childhood! In that case, anyone can be a genius!"

But no matter how much I thought about it, I didn't have an answer to my question: just what exactly am I? No matter how badly the desire to become a hero swelled inside me, I didn't know what I should do to realize my dream. After all, I was in elementary school. Every time I looked at my classmates, always goofing around, I envied their innocence. How nice it would've been to not have to think about what you are!

Eventually, I forgot about my philosophical dilemma and starting goofing around more than anyone else in my class.

That's pretty much how the years went by until, soon enough, I was ten years old and in fourth grade. And while I had been just messing around with my classmates all the time, I had kept asking myself the same thing: just what exactly am I? The only way in which I had grown, if at all, was moving up from *CoroCoro Comic* to *Shonen Jump*.

On one of those days, at one particular moment, my life changed. The fall term had just started. I was in homeroom. My mind was occupied by what might be on the cafeteria lunch menu.

Then my teacher spoke up.

"All of the fourth graders will be participating in this year's school play," she said.

Huh?

School play?

In second and third grade, there hadn't been a school play, only a chorus show. What was going on? When I listened to the rest of the teacher's explanation, I realized that at my school, starting in fourth grade, the entire class put on a play. Which meant that last year, the kids that were a year above me would have also put on a play in the gymnasium and we would've gone to see it. But for some reason, I couldn't remember it at all. I must not have been paying attention, because I was always joking around with my friends. I remembered that my teacher had gotten mad at me and made me stand in the corner facing the wall for a while.

So that's what had happened. But now I was intrigued.

"This year we'll be performing *The Naked King*. We talked about it last week, but since we'll be deciding on the cast today, please raise your hand if there is a role that you want to play," my teacher told us.

She told us last week? I really didn't remember. During last week's homeroom I had been busy conducting research on whether or not a rubber eraser would still work properly if you mixed one-part eraser with three-parts booger.

So that explained it! I watched my teacher and gave her a big nod.

For some reason my teacher was looking at me with a worried expression, but when I patiently smiled and gave her a thumbs up, she smiled back at me. When she got mad, she had a face like one of those horned demon masks. But typically, she was a gentle, kind teacher. She started to write the roles on the blackboard, with the crisp, satisfying scrape of the chalk.

Lead - King (1).

Tailors (4), Retainers (8), Servants (8), Villagers (10), and so on.

I absentmindedly watched her write the roles down, with my eyes particularly trained on the word "lead." I was very interested in being the King.

Lead! What an awesome word! I thought. *Hmm. But it's so embarrassing to ask to be the lead in front of everyone.*

For some reason my mind started to feel a bit hazy. My head and my chest felt like they were wrapped in clouds, crowded in by thick fog. I felt pain. I was breathless. I remembered that geniuses in books were usually frail and weak. I had never even caught a cold before, so maybe I was suddenly catching geniusitis! I decided to go all in on my feeble condition, and purposefully let out a violent coughing fit. One of my classmates slapped me on the back.

I heaved and hacked and ahemmed like never before! Usually, if someone were to slap me on the back, I would've shouted at them, "What the heck!" and shoved them in the chest. But I was supposed to be suffering from geniusitis, so I kept in character and turned around looking as frail as I could.

When I turned around, no one was there. I sat in the back row, after all. There were only the lockers and a plump red goldfish circling endlessly in a fish tank. In the glass, I could see my own face, my mouth a round 'O' of surprise.

Had I slapped myself?

In that moment, I nearly wet my pants. The face in the glass—that I had thought was my own—suddenly jumped out at me!

A face, then arms, and then the whole body of a middle-aged man pulled himself out of the fishbowl.

"Yo."

To fourth-grade me, he was just about the coolest hallucination imaginable.

But I didn't wet myself or even scream—I even surprised myself by how I simply accepted his sudden appearance. I was confused, but for some reason I wasn't scared.

He had big, goggling eyes. A large, serpentine nose. His hair was half-grown out, sloppily cut like he did it himself at whatever length suited him. He wore an old red cloak that almost looked like an Indian tunic. I felt like I had seen him somewhere before.

Was he one of the people who lived near the park I always went to play at?

"Not quite," he said.

It was as if he could hear my thoughts! Then he slapped me over the head. It hit me with a powerful slam, as if his fingers buried into my scalp like a hammer's blow.

"Ouch!" I cried.

"It was supposed to hurt," he said. "Are you awake now?"

"Huh? Is… is this a dream?"

"That's not an answer. I was asking if *you* were awake now, wasn't I?"

"Who-who are you, mister?"

I was scared so I decided to be polite.

The man raised his eyebrows and continued to stare at me. Then he suddenly glanced past me toward the blackboard and nodded in approval.

"I'm the King . . . that has a nice ring to it, doesn't it?" He smiled to himself like a little kid. "That's right. Call me King."

King? Was he crazy?

He did appear to be Japanese, after all, and, if anything, he looked more like King Kong.

As soon as I had the thought, he slapped my head again. Hard.

"King Kong? You moron. Call me *King*. You can add mister if you want," he said.

The man folded his arms and waited for my response. For a while I didn't know what to say, and then, finally, resigning myself, I said his name.

". . . King."

"There we go. Not bad, not at all. All right then, I'm King. I . . . am King. So tell me. Who are you?"

"Huh?" I responded.

"What are you? What do you want to be?"

"Wait—what?"

He had gotten to the very heart of my struggle as a genius. He knew what I feared most—the thing I had never told anyone.

The man, no, King, watched my troubled expression and let out a sigh.

"You're no fun, kid," he said.

All of the sudden he dunked his hand into the fish tank, scooped up a goldfish, and dropped it into his mouth with a gulp.

"W-wait a minute!"

"Wait what? What are we waiting for?" the man asked.

I didn't know what to say.

"You wanted me to wait because if that goldfish dies, then that cute girl in your gym class, Kayoko, would be devastated. That's why you wanted me to wait, right? Or do you just like goldfish that much? Is it because you love goldfish, it would be terrible for me to eat one? Is that why? Have you ever even fed a goldfish before?"

I was silent.

"But no, that's not it, either. Your little 'wait a minute' was just a common reaction. Am I wrong?"

I felt like I more or less understood what he was saying, but he was going too fast for me to keep up.

"Keep up with me! You're supposed to be a genius, after all."

King grinned.

"You can be lost. You can be confused. If there's something you want to ask, ask it. If there's something you want to say, say it. But don't be held captive to something as absurd as common sense. If you're held captive by that, you may as well not even bother speaking at all. Got it?"

King shook his head several times and rubbed his closed right fist over his mouth. When he opened his fist, I saw the goldfish in his palm, still alive. He dropped it back in the tank.

So he was a magician?

"Kid, you ever hear of Dragon Quest?" he asked.

"Of course I have."

"In Dragon Quest, you choose your profession, right?"

"Yeah! Isn't that obvious?"

"Obvious, huh? So you can choose whether to be a hero, a soldier, a priest, a mage, a Gadabout—anything you want, right?"

"That's right." I paused. "Does that mean—King, are you a mage?"

Completely ignoring my question, King continued.

"So how is Dragon Quest different from real life?"

Huh? Just as I was about to say *of course* Dragon Quest is different from real life because it's a *game,* I looked at King. His gaze was bearing down right on me. His mouth in a grin, his eyes laughing.

He was telling me to forget about common sense—that it's *not* different just because it's a game. That's when I was struck by lightning.

It was more like my body reacted *as if* I had been struck by lightning. It was a force even stronger than when King had hit me. It cut right through my fourth-grade self.

That's it!

"I get it!"

I said it out loud to King without thinking. He was standing

there waiting for my answer as if this was a trial. I looked excitedly at King and said my answer as boldly as I could.

"Ten years from now, when I become an adult, I can decide
my role in real life! Not just a role in a school play. I can be a
CEO, a politician, an artist, a businessman, a grocer, a tailor, an
athlete, or anything! All of my classmates and I are all going to
become adults someday, and we have to choose our own future.
And if that's true . . ."

King nodded for me to continue.

"And if that's true, then I can be whatever I want. Right
now. Starting now! And ten years from now, even when I become an adult, I can choose to be whatever I want to be, right?
No matter what anyone says to me. Even if they tell me I'm not
being realistic!"

Now I understood what King was saying when he asked
me if I was awake. If I really wanted to be one of the heroes
like in my manga, then I should become a hero. I had to make
my own choices. Just like Dragon Quest, I could choose my
favorite character—I just had to press my own start button.

King was watching me with a serious expression.

"That's what they call selfishness," he said. "Ego."

"What?"

Selfishness? I shouldn't be selfish. Don't be selfish.

I heard the expression buzzing around my ears. All of the
sudden I felt upset, like I had been rejected. I thought King had
been my friend, but he completely burst my bubble.

"Listen to me all the way through," he said.

I didn't know what he was talking about. But he spoke his next words slowly and clearly:

"Do what your ego says."

I watched him.

"If you decide who you are, you become who you decide to be. Your ego, your decision. You are your decisions. You are your ego." He paused. "Hm, well, this might be hard for a kid to understand."

"It's not hard. I get it!" I said.

"Don't get cheeky with me."

"No—I get it! More than anything else, I am my own ego! And in order to become my ego, I have to try my hardest. If I do what my ego says when I become an adult, I should be able to become whatever I want to be. That's what you mean, don't you, King?"

King chuckled like some kid who had just pulled off an amazing prank.

I felt like I was closer than ever to solving the question that had haunted me. From now on, I decided to listen only to my truest voice, my ego. If my friends were devoted to studying and sports, I would devote myself to my own ego! And as an occasion to celebrate the discovery of my ego, there was something I had to do—right now, today, in homeroom!

I turned back to the blackboard. They were staring at me—my teacher, my classmates, everyone. Or were they staring at King?

When I turned around no one was there anymore. There was only the fish tank and the goldfish, swimming in circles as always. But when I saw my face reflected in the glass, my eyes were on fire. Even the goldfish looked happy. I had escaped from the tank! I was so excited that I felt like even taiyaki fish-shaped pancakes could swim. And even goldfish could fly!

King had vanished like a ghost. I thanked him from the bottom of my heart. Then I faced my teacher and raised my hand.

"I want to be the lead!" I declared.

My teacher and classmates looked surprised. But as the sole student standing up, adrenaline pumping through my body, I started ranting about how only I was suited to play the role of King.

The class burst out in amused chatter.

"Wouldn't it be hilarious if the naked king was actually naked?" I said.

And at that there were responses of: "Yeah, I suppose so."

But everyone was tilting their heads to the side, still unsure.

"Is there anyone here that would be willing to play the king naked in front of everyone?" I challenged.

Everyone shook their heads quickly.

"Then I'll do it," I said. "I can do it, right?"

By pushing for what I wanted, I actually got the role of the Naked King. The lead!

"But it's a joke, right? About you being naked?" my teacher whispered anxiously.

But her words went right over my head. When I stripped myself butt-naked and exposed myself to the entire class in the pursuit of proving myself worthy, she gave me a good scolding.

"No matter what, *do not* take off your clothes at the actual performance!" she said, advising me to just pretend.

The day of the performance came, with all of the students and parents in attendance. I knew that I was supposed to pretend. But it sounded so fun that I couldn't help myself.

In a feverish, unforgettable performance, I became the true butt-naked king. I got a lot of laughs, a lot of scoldings, and it was a mess in general, but I didn't feel embarrassed at all.

I honestly thought that in order to pull off the performance, I had no choice but to truly become the Naked King.

Naturally, I was also chosen as the lead in the fifth-grade play and even the sixth-grade play, after I changed schools. I started to call myself the "Three-Time Consecutive Elementary School Play Leading Role Champion." The curtain had risen on the birth of my legendary ego.

The only time I ever saw King in elementary school was the day that I was chosen as the Naked King. I got the sense that he attended the performance, but I was in such a state of excitement that I have little memory of that night.

After the school play finished, summer vacation came fast. My big plans to goof off kept me quite occupied all summer long. Then, on the final day of summer vacation, I did all of my summer assignments in one fell swoop and paraded into class with a glorious sunburn. Sometime along the way, King had faded to a distant memory. I hardly remembered his face.

Then, another turning point came.

It was my sixth-grade summer vacation. My parents had told me suddenly that we were moving, and I was changing schools. We were going to South America—to the Republic of Chile.

Of course, I had no idea what kind of country Chile was, what kind of people lived there, or even what language they spoke.

So what's the problem?

For the first time in a while, I remembered King. I had a feeling that he would say something like that. Honestly, I felt the same way he did: *South America is different, but people are the same. The language is different, but I know that you can find your voice. And no matter what they tell you, continue to do whatever you want—even if it's a pointless struggle.*

My name—Yohei Kitazato. Profession—an egotistical little brat. Thanks to my meeting with King, I was determined to keep my leading role as the hero no matter the adventure ahead. And before my next adventure to Chile, without putting even the slightest thought into preparations, my heart was pounding in my chest.

This book is a story about protecting your ego time and time again; about never giving up on the pointless struggle of achieving every dream you've ever had. It's the story of an idiot genius who is always the star of his own show.

Chapter Two
A BOUT OF STRENGTH

My dad told me we were moving, I blinked, and we were in Chile.

South America. The Republic of Chile! The official language was Spanish, as it turned out.

My dad was employed by a trading firm, so transfers were common. But it was my first experience abroad.

Right at the height of summer, we took a wobbling thirty-hour flight from Narita Airport to Santiago Airport in Santiago, Chile. It looked like a modest airport—it was nothing compared to Narita. Outside the big windows, I saw a bright blue sky. When I went outside and sucked in the air of this new land, I found that it smelled and tasted totally different from Japan. I heard lively Spanish bouncing around the airport halls. I saw Chileans—people with dark skin, black hair, and a little shorter than I was used to. I still had no idea what kind of country Chile was, and I still didn't understand a lick of Spanish.

But from the moment that I landed in this unknown country, I decided that every single day was going to be an interesting one. The air felt comfortable on my skin, as if I had Latin American blood running through me. I didn't know if it was just how it was supposed to feel when you get to a foreign country, but I felt the purest sense of liberation.

I'm free!

I wanted to shout and start running as fast as I could.

While my mom and older sister tried to calm me down, we went through immigration, bowing politely to the well-armed soldiers, past the rows of open-air shops full of hand-crafted statues like the photos I had seen of Easter Islands, and out past customs, where we met up with my dad. My dad told me I looked pretty excited for having just gone on a thirty-hour flight, a tired smile on his face.

On our way to our new home in Santiago, I had my face glued to the car window, eyes trained on the new world passing by. Everything was fresh and exciting.

I was able to spend several months getting accustomed to my new life in Chile. I was enrolled in a school for Japanese ex-pats. But it was a tiny school with just six students in my entire year. There was no competition and I had far too much free time. Soon enough I couldn't bear it anymore, so we decided that I would transfer to a local school.

I realized most foreign schools really do start in September, not April. And the graduation was in June. So that meant I was starting my first semester of sixth grade in September.

It was my first day at my new school. It was called Nido de Aguilas, an international school for K–12. The school's name meant "Eagle's Nest" in Spanish.

Hmm. So it meant that they were raising eagles here, then, I thought. I pictured in my head a school full of eagle-headed humans and thought it was just about the coolest thing ever. *Awesome,* I thought, *I can become an eagle, too!* I saw myself transform into a mighty eagle and burst out of the walls of the school.

Nido de Aguilas was a bouncy, thirty-minute bus ride from my house. We rode up a hill to a wide lot of one-storied buildings spread over a gentle slope. From the looks of it, there seemed to be an open-minded atmosphere at the school. Rather than the brown wooden chairs of Japan that taste just a little sweet if you lick them, the classrooms had plastic desks with the chairs attached.

People even raised their hands differently. Like trying to hail a taxi, they just raised their hand and index finger straight up. No one shouted *"Hai!"* as they raised their hand. It was the cool, silent way to raise your hand.

I was taken aback by how different everything was from Japan, especially English class. Of course, it was all gibberish to me. I crossed my arms and looked around at my fellow classmates.

About half the class was from South America, either Chile or Argentina. Then in the other half there were blond-haired and blue-eyed students from America and Europe, as well as Asians too. Little baby eagles gathered from all around the world. Well, the first one to become an eagle would be none other than yours truly, I decided, firmly establishing my own superiority. I completely ignored the content of my classes.

Gym class was also different. We had no gym uniforms. Just a few of the girls changed into jerseys. Everyone wore whatever they wanted. I supposed that in Chile they simply didn't understand that clothes could get dirty.

Gym was also easy in Chile. After the teacher took attendance, he thought about it for a moment before saying: "All right, how about baseball today?"

He didn't mind ignoring the curriculum altogether. *Baseball, huh?* So that meant I had to be the star—pitcher, of course.

I was very determined to become the person who I wanted to be. I was a slave to my ego. With my glove in hand, I ambled over to the pitcher's mound. In my head, I was already deciding what to say to the press after being named the game's MVP.

But I wasn't the only one who went to the pitcher's mound. Other players were advancing on the mound as well. Including me, there were six candidates in total gathered at the mound. They were all South Americans: Chileans, a Brazilian, and an Argentinian. It was shaping up to be Team South America vs Team Japan, represented by me.

I was suddenly nervous. A quiet fell.

Then pandemonium broke out. All five of them were shouting, gesturing angrily, even shoving one other! I had no idea what they were saying other than "Let *me* be the pitcher!" I had never seen anything like this in Japan.

I realized how easy I had it in Japan. Back there, my ego was the top dog. But here in Chile—or maybe in South America more broadly—they had natural-born egos.

I couldn't stand losing!

I frantically fought back with gestures. But I had no idea what anyone else was saying, and they couldn't understand me either. I kept shouting "Let me be pitcher!" in Japanese over and over again, but they didn't even understand the word "pitcher." At first they glanced at me as if to say, "Who's this kid?" But soon enough Team South America started to ignore me all together.

It was as if there was a bubble of thick glass all around me. Even though I was talking right at them, I couldn't communicate anything at all. They weren't even letting me in the fighting ring. The bubble of glass had gone completely opaque. With even my gestures becoming futile, I stood totally petrified.

And because I didn't speak English or Spanish, I didn't have a single friend.

That was no reason to lose. And yet, in the duel of egos, I had to admit defeat.

Eventually, without saying a word, I resigned myself to the outfield, hardly better than a ball boy. My favorite parts of school, gym and recess, were obliterated before my very eyes. I just wasted the day away until school came to an end.

I thought to myself, *So my ego only works in the tiny island of Japan, huh?*

On the way home in the lively school bus, alone, I stared at my reflection in the window. That was no young, growing eagle that I saw. I remembered that old saying, "The frog in the well knows nothing of the great ocean." I was the frog, not an eagle.

There was chatter and laughter surrounding me. But over the course of that bus ride, I started to see my fellow students as no different from kids in Japan. The mixture of English and Spanish started to even sound like Japanese.

But I felt like everyone was saying, "That Asian kid is so full of himself. At least now he's sitting there quietly."

Even though I'm normally really good at comebacks, if they couldn't understand what I said, it didn't matter anyway. When I remembered how the boys on the pitcher mound were speaking as fast as machine gun fire, with my broken English and few words of Spanish, I knew I didn't even have a shot at communication with them.

For Japanese people living in a Spanish-speaking country, I remembered hearing that it took two years to become proficient. Two years. I would have to seal my ego away for two years before unleashing it again. I would have to become one of the people who just sat there and listened to what others told them.

That sucked.

And what about my fellow Japanese classmates who were already on the sidelines?

They were all pointing at me, laughing, saying, "Now you're just like the rest of us."

Damn it! Damn it all!

Overwhelmed with frustration and pain, I clenched my fists until they hurt. I didn't what to do with them.

Gong! Whack!

I heard a dull sound and felt a sharp pain at the back of my head. When I turned to see, I bumped my forehead against the window.

It was a pain sandwich. Not an unfamiliar pain though. I heard someone quietly humming Seiko Matsuda's song "Sweet Memories."

When I turned around, it wasn't Seiko Matsuda behind me, of course, but King.

"Hola. ¿Como está?"

King was speaking to me in Spanish.

Yo. How's it going? It was the only Spanish I knew, but I didn't even know how to respond. I looked at King.

This time he wore an Andean robe. He had a South American vibe, but also that same homeless man vibe he had from the first time I met him. I wondered when he had come to Chile. His suntanned face and easygoing attitude made him look basically like a Chilean. In this South American country where I didn't have a single friend in the world, at last, there was someone I knew.

King opened his arms, and without the slightest sign of embarrassment, I tried to jump into them.

Smack!

He slapped my cheeks with both hands.

"Dozing off again, aren't you?"

More than a reunion, this was going to be a sermon.

"I've wanted to tell you for a long time," I said, "but your slaps *hurt*. They're not a joke, they're violent!"

Completely ignoring what I said, King continued.

"Hey, question for you. Why did you lose so easily?"

I glared at him. "I couldn't even speak to them!"

"Couldn't even this, couldn't even that. You're still a little kid."

"I tried my best to talk to them—"

"And it wasn't enough, right? Quit with the excuses. If you didn't get it done, that's the end of the story, isn't it?"

I couldn't find words to respond. I knew he was right.

"Hey, do you like Big G?"

"Huh?"

"Big G. From *Doraemon*. You know what I'm talking about."

I thought about it. Big G is a big, tough character that rules the neighborhood by force. "Well, I don't love him, but I don't hate him either. He was good in the *Doraemon* movie."

"Right. So what do you think Big G would do if he was in Chile?"

"Huh?"

"If Big G came to Chile, do you think he'd just stay quiet if he couldn't speak the language? You think he'd just hold back?"

"But Big G's from a manga—"

As soon as I started to say it, I felt another sharp pain to my forehead. King had flicked me. He sure had a repertoire of attacks, and they all hurt. But the flick opened my eyes up in a few ways. It reminded me to forget about "common sense." Of course, since Big G was in a manga, it was common sense that he wouldn't come to Chile. But still, I didn't want to be like Big G, who simply got everything he wanted with overwhelming force. If there was a fight, I wouldn't run from it, but I didn't want to start fights either. I didn't want to hurt people weaker than me.

"That's right," King said. "Big G is bad because he bullies and takes advantage of those weaker than him with force. That's lame. But like you said, Big G could be a pretty cool guy. And that . . ."

"That's because other times he fights alongside people weaker than him?"

King nodded.

"He takes risks in order to protect his friends."

"Which means . . . ?" I asked.

"Which means . . . ?" King repeated.

"Well, it's just that I don't even know who's weaker than me in my class," I said. "I don't have friends, either."

King erupted into a stream of violent curses. His forceful Spanish was completely unintelligible. I understood a little bit at the end, but they weren't expressions worth writing down in a novel. They were all filthy words.

"You really make excuse after excuse for yourself, you spoiled brat.

Let's think about it as simply as possible.

First things first. Do you think you can really just wait for two years until you become fluent in Spanish?

Also, isn't there a way to use strength without hurting others? Win with your strength rather than your words.

And last but not least, whether or not there are other people you need to protect, whether or not you even have friends, you still have to protect your own pride!

No matter what, don't accept defeat so damned easily!"

It was like he had struck my head with a giant hammer.

Last time it was a thunderbolt. This time, a deep, heavy blow rippled across my body.

Since I had last seen King in fourth grade, I had gone on protecting my ego without any skills to speak of, only my mouth. But there would be enemies I couldn't take down like that. Now I had met opponents that were bigger and stronger.

Mere words would have no effect. But this was no time to make that an excuse.

If your first weapon doesn't work, then what do you do? If a copper sword doesn't cut, go to a steel sword. I needed to challenge them without the power of my words. I needed the power of a universal language.

I knew I could do it. I wouldn't lose anymore. Being patient for one day was more than enough. To hell with patience.

"Say it again?" King grinned as he asked.

To hype myself up, I responded with a shout.

"To hell with patience!"

I realized all of the sudden that I was standing in the middle of the bus with my fists in the air. Everyone was watching me blankly.

Up until now, no one had cared about me whatsoever. I had been invisible to them. But that was the moment that I caught their attention. Now that I had it, I grinned and introduced myself with the only Spanish I knew: "Hola! ¿Como está?"

Starting the next day, I became a warrior.

I began to challenge the mighty egos of Team South America. While throwing plenty of provocative gestures their way, I challenged them to bouts of manly strength—arm wrestling.

Since there were kids who got bored of just doing arm wrestling, we established a rule that the winner got to punch the loser in the shoulder however hard he wanted.

It's harder than you think to actually punch another person with all of your strength. Still, a punch to the shoulder doesn't hurt so bad, so the losers didn't mind it much. The nastiest rascals of us all loved this game the most. We played during recess, in between classes, whenever we could. Of course, even if I lost, I kept playing until I won. I believed that if you eventually won, then you were no longer a loser.

A year passed. Every single day felt more jam-packed than my busiest day in Japan. Over the course of that year, I managed to restrain the egos of my South American classmates by sheer force (arm wrestling). When arm wrestling didn't settle matters, in the case of a stronger classmate, I picked fights.

During these bouts of strength (rudimentary fistfights), I also improved my communication skills. I started to be able to speak conversational English and Spanish. I continued to assert my ego and got into plenty of arguments.

My classmates always told me, "Yohei, you're too selfish!"

"The most selfish kid in the class is that Japanese boy," they said.

To me, those words were a medal of honor.

I acted the same way outside of class too. Right near the school, there was a poor neighborhood of small black houses.

When I got on the bus it was no problem, but if I missed the bus I had to walk home through the neighborhood.

In Chile at the time, discrimination and prejudice were problems. Every time I walked through the town, large numbers of small kids gathered and yelled "Chino!" and even threw rocks at me. It's not that they hated Chinese people in particular, but they didn't know the difference between Asian countries and scornfully called any Asian a Chino. But after about a year of experiencing this, whenever a kid threw a rock at me, I picked up an even bigger rock and hurled it back. I grew so much in that one year!

I didn't see King for the rest of the year. Since that day that we met on the bus, there were so many things I wanted to ask him. *Why were you in Chile? What exactly are you? When can I see you again?* Above all, I wanted to tell him how I had started to have fun in Chile, no matter the situation.

Instead of telling King, I decided to write a letter to my Japanese classmates back home. It was a letter that I had been too afraid to write before, from the very first day of classes and our induction ceremony in the Nido de Aguilas gymnasium, all the way up until now. The letter read:

It's been a while. How are you? I'm the definition of awesome over here. South America really isn't that different from Japan anyway. I'm having tons of fun.

From,

Big G in Chile

Chapter Three
THE ANYWHERE DOOR

If I had to explain the South American character in one sentence, I would say: South Americans are overflowing with passion. If I could add another sentence, it would be: there are a lot of show-offs. It's good to stand out in Chile.

And then to add one final sentence: everybody loves soccer.

No matter the era, soccer players are South American heroes. But the most popular of them all are the ace strikers—because they show off the most. In Chile, all the kids want to play forward and become national heroes. Pele, Maradona, Ronaldinho, and Messi are all ace strikers.

Goalkeepers can be heroes, sometimes. The Colombian goalkeeper Higuita used to go all the way from his own goal to score on the opposing team.

At the World Cup, the biggest stage in soccer, Maradona even scored a goal with his hand. After the match he said the goal was scored "a little with his head, a little with the hand of God." Of course, in Japan illegal plays are booed, but it met thunderous applause in South America. People even began to praise the goal, and it became known as the "hand of God," a legendary goal worthy of praise.

Soccer players reigned in Chilean society as the kings of showing off. They were good team players as well, but their style was fundamentally selfish. I also loved the fiery support of the fans. South American soccer was the very thing I had been searching for.

When I transferred to Nido de Aguilas, I bumped up against a wall—the language barrier—but eventually I managed to overcome it thanks to King. After that, even though I aspired to be Big G, my interest in baseball waned, and I devoted myself to soccer instead.

Soccer helped me stand out, and it helped me protect my ego too. Even though I was unskilled, I could cover the opponent with relentless intensity.

Soccer was the perfect fit. I was completely on board.

And thanks to soccer, I discovered the Anywhere Door.

In Chile, there's a soccer team called Colo-Colo. It was Santiago's club team and the team emblem was the profile of an Indigenous chief. When the Spanish first invaded Chile, the heroic local Mapuche tribe never gave up fighting back. So the team was named Colo-Colo after the Mapuche chief.

Perhaps because of this historical influence, Colo-Colo had an offensive, aggressive style of play. They were at the peak of their strength from the 1980s all the way until the 1990s. In 1991 they ascended to the top of the soccer world, eventually defeating the Brazilian team in the 1992 Recopa Sudamericana, and becoming the number one team in South America. They even came to Japan for the Intercontinental Cup once. When I was in Chile, they were the best of the best.

As I devoted myself to soccer, I found myself, like the rest
of Chilean soccer lovers, a huge fan of Colo-Colo. It was the
first time I had been a fan of anyone. Up until then, I hadn't
been interested in the stars on TV. I always thought, what's the
point of being obsessed with someone you don't even know?
But just by watching the Colo-Colo matches, my body got hot
and I found myself screaming whenever something dramatic
happened.

I loved all of the players on Colo-Colo, but Gabriel Coca
Mendoza the most of all. I loved his intense long hair and his
sharp eagle eyes. He was strong and quick, and played like a
wild animal. I went countless times to cheer him on at the stadium, but even that wasn't enough for me, so I recorded all
of his plays on video and watched them by myself over and
over again, and memorized every play of the game. Sometimes
I ran into plenty of issues, like running out of videotape or
getting the videocassette stuck in the player—like how my high
school male classmates would get porn videocassettes stuck in
their players from watching them over and over again. But no
matter how many times I watched and rewatched the videos, I
knew that watching it live for the first time was by far the most
exciting.

Two years had passed since I moved to Chile. I was in my
second year of middle school. One day at the Santiago soccer stadium, Colo-Colo was playing Universidad de Chile, their

biggest rival. Tickets sold out in the blink of the eye. After shedding countless tears, I watched the match at home with my best friend, Pampi.

It was a fierce match. As the game went on, my excitement grew and grew. Basically clinging to the television every time Colo-Colo scored a goal, we went absolutely wild.

"GOOOOOOOOOOOOLLLLL! GOLAZO!"

Golazo means "super goal" in Spanish. By that time, I had nearly mastered all of the Spanish words relating to soccer, and when it came to slang, I was basically a native speaker.

After that amazing goal, Colo-Colo finally took control of the match. It was tense. We screamed and roared at the TV.

So many war cries at the screen was making my voice hoarse.

Later that night, I was in bed, still wide awake from all the excitement. One of my best talents was falling asleep as soon as I got into bed, but that night I couldn't even close my eyes. I felt like my head was on fire and I could hear my heart beating in my chest.

I turned on the light and opened the window. A chilly breeze blew in through the window and I could see stars glittering in the night sky. In Japan, you couldn't see this many stars unless you went deep into the countryside. I tried to identify constellations, but all I could see were soccer balls—soccer balls made of stars.

At school recess, we played soccer.

When school let out, I went to the nearest park to play soccer with locals.

On the weekends, I watched soccer on TV.

And even though I was completed immersed in soccer, for some reason I wasn't satisfied. I didn't understand why. I sighed with all the passion of a lover looking at the night sky and making a wish. But the moment I sighed, my instincts screamed out.

He's coming!

It was too late. I felt a sharp kick hit my ass, and I leapt up in pain. I jolted so far forward that I nearly fell out the window. Our apartment was on the eighteenth floor, high above a concrete parking lot. I nearly joined the stars in the sky that night.

When I looked behind me, I saw King, who for some reason was wearing a Colo-Colo uniform. A soccer ball lay at his feet. So King was into soccer too. No wonder the kick hurt so bad.

"I nearly fell out the window!" I yelled.

"If you're going to sigh like that, maybe a good fall is what you need to wake up."

Come on, King. If I fell out this window, I'd be dead—no more waking up. (I made sure that my replies were kept to myself.)

"Don't sigh like that!" King said. "You want something, but you can't get it, right? But I don't know what you're sighing for. Are you praying to Buddha for your salvation? What will sighing

do about it? Are you going to ask the stars for help? Will the
star goddess come down and save you? No chance in hell! They
ain't coming! You want what you want, sure. And to get it, your
ego wants it so badly it could die. Then get it, of your own will!
Aren't you the type of person who gets what he wants? What
the hell?! You're just sitting in bed moaning and groaning and
groaning and moaning. You're going to look at that twinkling
starry sky and just *sigh*? You're playing the dreamy-eyed girl?
You exhaust me, you moron!"

Then he started to juggle the soccer ball. He completely
ignored me, as if to leave me in peace to sigh like a dreamy-eyed
girl.

I was like a goalkeeper just standing there spacing out during a penalty kick. Even though I knew the kicks were coming,
King continued to nail his shots with perfect accuracy. King
always showed up at a time I wanted to deal with him the least.

Frustrated, I tried to steal the ball from King, but he directed it away. Every time I jumped at him to swipe the ball, he
evaded me effortlessly. All of my confidence in my soccer skills,
carefully built over two years, suddenly cracked and shattered.
I was shaken. I lost to King, every time. I went after him hard,
but King played dirty, grabbing and pulling my clothes. Somehow King was perfectly familiar with South American soccer.

Before I realized it, I was covered in sweat, staggering like
a toddler. And then, suddenly my legs tangled, and I toppled
over. I couldn't think. The world around me was white.

The chilly breeze blew in through the window. I closed my eyes and felt the cold on my skin.

"I want to be on the field with Mendoza . . ." I mumbled.

"Yes! *Goooooal!*" King lined up a powerful kick and shot the ball through the open window. We heard the distant clang of the ball against a building a few houses down the street.

"That's your ball," King said.

"What?"

I didn't have the energy to get up. Whatever, I thought.

"So what you really want finally came out," King said.

"What?"

"Play," he said.

"Play what?"

"Play soccer!"

"We just played. And now you lost my ball!"

"Don't be stupid! You said you want to play *with* Mendoza! So, challenge him to a match!"

King had forced me to face what I really wanted. And that was to run and play alongside my favorite players. I wanted to play with them at that sacred stadium, at Estadio Monumental. But I wasn't a pro soccer player, so I had figured it was obvious that I'd never be able to do it.

"How stupid," King said. "'Obvious' doesn't mean anything to me."

As always, King saw right through me.

"You don't need to be a pro to play soccer with someone!"

I had no idea what he was getting at, but I nodded.

That night, I stayed up late with King and devised a strategy:

1. Write a letter of challenge to Mendoza. 2. Go to the next Colo-Colo game at Estadio Monumental. 3. After the game, climb over the fence and run on to the field. 4. Race to the players before the guards catch me. 5. Give the letter of challenge to Mendoza. 6. Get caught by the guards. 7. Wait for Mendoza's response. 8. Get summoned to play at Estadio Monumental and have the match of my dreams!

It was the perfect plan. My heart danced to a Latin beat. King and I shook hands and slapped each other on the back.

Mind and body completely exhausted, I dove into bed. I plopped my head on the pillow and just before I fell asleep, a simple question floated to mind. Managing to raise my head from my beloved pillow, I looked over at King. For some reason he was practicing Japanese soccer player Kazuyoshi Miura's famous victory dance.

"I just thought of one thing," I said to him.

King stopped dancing. "What is it?"

"I just realized that every time I meet you it's when I'm looking at my reflection, like in a mirror or a window or something. The first time it was the fish tank. The second time, the school bus window. Both times I was looking at my reflection. I thought maybe it had something to do with that, but this time was different."

"What, did you think I was some fairy that only popped out of windows or something?"

You're not exactly cute or fairy-like, I wanted to tell him.

"No, not that . . ."

"I can come from anywhere," King said. "*But.*"

"But what?"

"Whenever you're in a bad situation, you tend to be looking at mirrors and windows."

I almost never looked in the mirror. I didn't care about my hairstyle or anything. I couldn't even become friends with the type of person who was always looking at themselves in the mirror. But whenever I was lost, or confused about what to do, it was true that I tended to look into mirrors or out windows.

"I see . . ." I vaguely understood. "One more thing, King."

"You said just one thing before, didn't you?" King asked. "Real men keep their word." His words slammed against me.

I decided to give up on the second question. I told myself that solving the puzzle of how he appeared was enough.

In the future, once I was working, if I had a job that

required me to shave every morning, what would I think about having to look in the mirror every day? Starting to think about that put me right to sleep.

The next day during lunch break at school I gathered the Colo-Colo fans I knew from class and told them about the perfect plan King and I had crafted. I figured that they'd burst into applause.

But they all rejected it.

"Impossible," they said.

According to my classmates, first of all, the fence between the spectators and the field at Estadio Monumental was ridiculously high. On top of that, the ridiculously tall fence was covered in barbed wire. But even if you leapt over the top like some kind of ninja, there were tons of guards gathered in between the fence and the field.

"Yeah, but I won't know if I don't try," I argued.

Just as I started to make my point, they all changed the topic of conversation. Even my closest friend Pampi gave me a shrug, like I was a foreigner that they couldn't bother to understand. Well, I *was* a foreigner, but still.

They may have all rejected my plan, but I really wouldn't know until I tried. If I went to the game, maybe somehow I could make it happen. I was a genius after all, so I had a positive attitude. I bought tickets to the very next Colo-Colo game at Estadio Monumental.

On the day that I was to put my plan into action, I arrived at the stadium early. The stadium itself was so impressive that it almost made the trip worth it. I felt like I could go home right then and still be satisfied. But I shook my head and headed off to my seat.

I ran into a passionate group of Colo-Colo fans called Gala Blanca, who were shouting fight songs at the top of their lungs. The stadium was rocking with excitement, even though the start of the game was still far off.

When the match began, a new level of intensity enveloped the stadium. The bellow of a low drum rumbled in my gut. Gala Blanca matched their chanting and jumping to the drum's rhythm. Every time they jumped, it felt like the earth shook under my feet.

So this was Estadio Monumental! South American soccer was nothing short of epic. The aggressive play of the team, the passionate chanting of Gala Blanca—together they created a wild enthusiasm that swept over the entire stadium. Sure, other stadiums might have their own atmospheres, but this was different. Covered in goosebumps, I started to cheer with the crowd and totally forgot about myself and my own plans.

The game turned out to be a huge victory for Colo-Colo. My beloved Gabriel Coca Mendoza played like a star. More than the feeling from any other game I had seen before, this was the most satisfied I had ever felt. But I knew that my next match was just beginning.

No matter what happened, and no matter what means I needed to achieve my goal, I was determined to infiltrate the stadium and deliver my handwritten letter of challenge to Gabriel Coca Mendoza.

ESTADIO MONUMENTAL VS THE INTRUDER.

The second match that nobody else knew about was about to begin.

I searched for some fence that looked possible to climb over, but there didn't seem to be any feasible location. There was no way anyone could get over that barbed wire without hurting themselves. My friends had warned me about that, so I wasn't too surprised. I stayed composed as I walked around the arena. There was no sign of any way to get onto the pitch.

What could I do? I thought about it as I finished my lap around the arena.

There is always a better way!

I knew there had to be. The players got to the field somewhere.

It had already been ten or twenty minutes since the game had ended. I was running out of time. Soon the players might end up leaving the stadium. I had to get Mendoza my letter of challenge, no matter what.

I abandoned my leisurely pace and sprinted across the

stadium, searching desperately for a solution. Then, at last I found it—the simplest, shortest possible route, free of fences, straight to the players. It was the players' entrance. Two guards guarding a single, big door.

My dream awaited me on the other side of that VIP entrance. It was like the Anywhere Door from *Doraemon*—the door that, when you walk through it, transports you to exactly where you want to be.

The first Anywhere Door that I found turned out to be one iron, heavy bastard. Even in *Doraemon* I didn't remember the Anywhere Door being this hard to use. I resolved myself to force this very intense, very real door wide open.

Let's go, ego! Time to make my dreams come true! My heart screamed as if summoning a magic spell.

Of course, I was no mage. So first, I decided to simply try to just walk through the door as if I had no idea what was going on.

As expected, the guards called out to me. Whenever a hero tries to make their dreams come true, there will always be monsters that appear to try to stop them. Games and reality were one and the same.

"Wait a second," called the monsters—I mean the guards, who incidentally had faces as ugly as monsters.

"Excuse me? What's the problem?" I answered innocently.

"Where do you think you're going?"

The other guards approached. They closed in on both sides of me. It was a good defensive position.

"I have something really important for the players," I responded, as if I were family.

The guards snorted.

"Listen up, our job here is to prevent the likes of you from getting in. That's why we're standing here. So turn around and walk away."

It was a fair point. It's over, I thought to myself, if you looked at the facts . . . I started to think, but the moment I turned my back to the door I felt a brutal kick to my ass, an even sharper pain than the one King had given me a few days ago.

When I turned around, gasping in pain, I saw that the face of one of the guards had turned into King's face. *If that was you the whole time, why don't you just let me in!* I screamed to myself. But King looked at me with a scornful grin, as if to say, *I'm not going to let this be easy.* The force of his glare was even more terrifying than the guards and I took several steps back.

"Listen up," King said. "The moment you think, 'it's a fair point, it's all over,' that's the moment you lose. Somewhere deep down, you figured you wouldn't be able to do it all along, didn't you? You'll never protect your ego if you think like that. Fight your pointless fight, won't you?!"

But no matter what he told me, I really didn't see any way

that I could win here. The other guards didn't appear to hear what King was saying. I didn't know if King's shirt was too tight or something, but for some reason he started undoing the buttons.

"I have no idea what you're dilly-dallying for," King said. "This is a simple situation. It's just you, who wants to get in, and the guards, who don't want you to get in. Whoever wants it more wins. It's as simple as that. Your feeling of wanting to get in is your selfishness. But the guards are here, they want to stop you, they want to do their job right and earn a salary and please their boss—that's their selfishness."

I suddenly understood. I felt it all snap into place.

This was a battle of egos.

"This sort of battle of wills has a single outcome," King said. "If you don't win, then they do. It's never over before it starts."

If my ego could emerge victorious, I'd be able to slay the monster. And I'd be able to get through the Anywhere Door and make my dream come true.

I was ready for round two. I slapped my own cheeks to get fired up. And as if on cue, the second guard's face went back to normal and King disappeared.

I got it, King. Thanks.

I turned and faced the monsters. I coughed lightly to clear my throat and narrowed my eyes.

"My dream is to go in there, give my letter of challenge to the players, and play a soccer match in front of everyone in this stadium," I said. "Can you please tell me why you would try to interfere with my dream?"

The guard responded like I was being an unreasonable child.

"I told you already, our job is to stop kids like you from getting in."

The last time he told me that, it knocked me out. But now I understood the rules of this fight. It wouldn't slow me down this time. I took a step closer. I looked up at the two guards, who loomed over me like beefy, human refrigerators.

"I moved to Chile from Japan two years ago. I'm Japanese. But in my time living in this passionate country, I've become passionate too. I'm passionate about making my dream come true. As Latinos, you understand that feeling, don't you?"

There was a small pause. "I don't see what that has to do with us letting you in."

The guards were thinking. Chileans, proud of the passionate, Latin blood running through their veins, called themselves Latino. They recognized this passion and made it a virtue, a part of their heritage. Certainly, they would be happy that a Japanese person recognized that about them. Now was my chance! I lined up my next argument.

"This is my only chance!" I begged. "If I don't go now,

I won't be able to make my dream come true. I understand why you don't want to let me through this door. You don't want your boss to get mad, but could you at least let a thirteen-year-old kid all the way from Japan make his dream come true? As Latinos, don't you want to support a kid's passion? All the Chileans I know always help me out! Well then, if you don't, you won't be very proud Latinos, would you?"

They were silent for a moment. I had said everything I wanted to say, and my throat was parched.

I swallowed. The guards looked at each other, then at me, and said sternly:

"We didn't see anything. Go."

It was a miracle!

My passion and the words I had come up with—they had chased off the monsters like magic spells. I pumped my fist as I opened up the Anywhere Door with two hands and rushed towards the field to make my dream come true.

The Anywhere Door was leading me to my beloved Colo-Colo players!

I trotted out through the hallway in search of the Colo-Colo players' changing room, rushed into it, and at last, I saw them.

The first person I saw was the player who had scored the

decisive goal of the championship match, the team representative and captain, Jaime Pizzaro. There was the captain of the Bolivian team, Marco Etcheverry, who had the nickname "El Diablo." There was leading Brazilian striker, Toninho. The vicious Chilean defender, Javier Margas. Then there was my favorite player, the Colo-Colo ace, Gabriel Coca Mendoza. I saw them and all the other players I so much admired.

Huh? Was there something else there too?

I rubbed my eyes. The toned, muscled bodies of my heroic soccer players, laughing and enjoying the taste of victory of their rival, were standing before me completely naked, dicks, balls, and all.

I certainly felt the difference in scale between the penises of these South American adults and those of the Japanese children I grew up with . . . but not ready to give up on my goal, I rushed between them, naked as they were, to Mendoza.

I quickly introduced myself as seriously as I could and handed him my official letter of challenge.

"Please accept my challenge!" I declared.

Mendoza looked surprised for a second, and then he smiled and gave me the OK sign. He'd do it!

I didn't hear this until later, but apparently I was the first to start a tradition of ordinary people sneaking into the Estadio Monumental to offer letters of challenge to players.

ESTADIO MONUMENTAL VS THE INTRUDER
WINNER: THE INTRUDER

I won the match!

A few days later, I was invited to Colo-Colo's practice at Estadio Monumental and got to play against all of my favorite players. A showdown. Me versus the best in the world—it was really a dream come true.

And best of all, they didn't treat me like a kid. They grabbed my uniform, went for the legs on their slide-tackles, and sent me flying, as if to tell me, "This is how the pros play, kid." They baptized me into the world of rough play. Even though our skill levels were far from even, it made me unbelievably happy to be on the same field and treated the same way as the best of the best.

I now understood that King was trying to do the same thing for me with his rough play in my room that night. No matter how many times I fell over, it was still fun. I played my heart out.

I ended up befriending the players. They seemed to appreciate that I was a weird kid all the way from Japan, and they ended up inviting me back to their practices several times afterward. Since the neighborhood around the stadium wasn't very safe at night, after practice the players even dropped me off at home.

When I told my friends at school, everyone's jaw dropped.

They had no choice but to recognize the brilliance of my plan. When they finally grasped the fact that the plan had been amazing, there was no jealousy or hard feelings. They just complimented me and enjoyed the story. I appreciated the good Latin attitude.

I was proud of myself, but above all, I was thrilled that I discovered the Anywhere Door. If you can open the Anywhere Door, it really will take you wherever you want.

Those Anywhere Doors were meant to be opened. And I could only open them with my own two hands.

Chapter Four
A LEGENDARY JOURNEY

I was fourteen years old, every day was hot, and I was having the time of my life. That's when I encountered destiny once again. This time it arrived in the form of a book.

It was a book that someone in our family had casually placed on the table. I discovered it one day after coming home from school. I had always been more of an exclusively manga reader, but for some reason this book attracted my attention and I started flipping through the pages. I saw that the book centered on the Chilean island of Chiloé. I hadn't heard of the place before. I sat on the sofa, and, struggling through the difficult words, started to read.

Chiloé was an island over 800 miles to the south from my home in Santiago. Originally, the entire island was covered in a dense forest, all nature and nothing else. Even after colonists cleared the land for settlements, plenty of forest remained, and the settlers subsided on the woods and the sea. Since long ago, the settlers had a simple life as farmers and fishers. The other constants were the fog and rain, the gray sky, the raging sea, the deep woods.

And about this island, cloaked in mystery, there were many myths and legends.

Normally I would give up on anything that wasn't a manga

after about three seconds, but soon I became completely ab-
sorbed.

There was La Viuda, the black-clothed widow that em-
braced men from behind in the depths of night, the titanic sea
lion that surfaced in the ocean, ghost ships, the Queen of the
Sea, warlocks and witches. Reading the book, tugged along by
the mystery and hints of eroticism, I felt something uncanny.
As a middle-schooler, I loved the feeling of reading a book
meant for adults.

I quickly called my friend Yuho. Yuho was another Japanese
boy who lived in Santiago and went to Nido de Aguilas, but he
was born in Peru and spoke fluent Spanish. Even though both
of his parents were Japanese, his face looked nearly Peruvian.

"Yuho, I found an awesome island." I told Yuho about all
of the new stories I had taken in, these legends of Chiloé. "Let's
go there," I proposed to him. "I want to see if the legends of
Chiloé are true or not! I want to see if La Viuda really grabs me
from behind!"

Yuho was also enchanted by the tales of Chiloé, and we
decided to go. I was so excited that the point of how we'd get
there never really came up.

It would be the first trip in my life by myself with only a
friend. That alone sent me trembling with excitement.

In order to make our plan to verify the legends of Chiloé, we convened a strategy meeting. Regarding the 800-mile

distance between Santiago and Chiloé, we took an optimistic outlook: if we just biked and hitchhiked, we'd have no problem getting there—eventually. We also needed a place to stay, but we had no money.

"Well, a tent is basically a portable hotel," I said.

"We can figure it out once we get there," Yuho agreed.

The meeting was concluded.

We didn't consider any of the specifics. Everything was going to be new to us—our first-ever trip without our parents. Without interference from adults, we'd have complete freedom. We'd become travelers, adventurers. Whenever I thought about it, my heart pounded with joy. But in order to make our trip a reality, we'd have to get around plenty of obstacles.

First were the parents.

I was fourteen and in my second year of middle school. We were in South America, which is not the safest region in the world. We had no idea what was beyond Santiago, let alone what would happen during the ridiculously long trip from Santiago to Chiloé. There isn't a parent in the world that would approve of our plan.

It was true that I was a spoiled kid. My parents were generous and kind. However, they had a strict side, too. Their anger could emerge, furious like the war god Ashuraman from the *Kinnikuman* wrestling manga. I'd kept their strictness hidden under a veil until now. Why, I don't know.

The leading representative of my household's strict side was none other than its head, my father. My father had a bulky, short stature, and a silent but forceful appearance. He had an aura about him that told me that I was *not* supposed to make him angry. And when he did get angry, it was honestly terrifying. I heard a countdown—*Three, two, one*—before he started blowing steam from his ears and shooting lasers out of his big dark eyes, under his thick, black eyebrows. No, not lasers, just a pressure intense enough to be felt across the room. He was a perfectionist that demanded that I get no less than the best grades in the class.

And since he was a top-class businessman, I couldn't even complain about his demands. He wasn't the type to talk about his work at home very often, so I didn't know the details, but I could read about his work in the newspaper pretty often and I saw once that he even shook hands with the President of Chile. I never thought that being a typical Japanese salaryman was lame, because I could see my dad in the newspaper, in his suit and tie, and thought it was the coolest thing in the world. Anytime I complained to my dad about something, he easily dismantled my argument.

I could see absolutely no way to get permission to go on my trip from my stern and argumentatively impenetrable father. Still, I had to get permission, somehow. Leaving without saying anything felt wrong.

Somehow, I had to climb over this wall. If I addressed him directly and honestly, maybe the Anywhere Door would appear and get me through.

"A legendary journey."

The catchphrase popped into my head and I couldn't get it out. We had to do something, so Yuho and I came up with a new plan—the Legendary Journey Presentation Conference Grand Strategy!

Part one—propose a camping trip with Yuho's family and mine; do not mention the legendary journey at all costs—was a success.

The day of the camping trip, things went smoothly. Our dads got to know each other better. We had a campfire going.

Our parents were sitting around the fire, chatting over glasses of wine, when we gathered the presentation material we had stealthily prepared. Then we presented our proposal to embark on our legendary journey.

But by the time the fire had gone out, our parents had completely extinguished our plan as well.

"You haven't thought this through at all."

"It's too dangerous!"

"You're still too young."

My mom, Yuho's parents, and both of our sisters raised

their various objections to our plan. We were barraged with a surround-sound system of rejection, coming from five speakers at once.

My dad alone kept his mouth shut. I suppose he figured that because the rest of the family was already beating us, the main boss didn't even need to show up.

Over the next several months, we tried again and again to convince our families to no avail.

"Why don't they understand?" we grumbled to each other.

No matter how many times we tried, and no matter how passionately we pled our case, the answer was always no.

I started to get upset. I felt like I was just spinning my wheels, getting angrier and angrier. If I just kept running on idle, I had no chance of convincing anyone to let us go on this legendary journey. I was no different than a whining child. Somewhere along the way I realized that this whole idea was leading me in a downward spiral. I kept falling, rushing further and further down. And it was a dead-end.

I stared at the wall in my bedroom. It was plastered with maps of Chile, countless photos, and articles about Chiloé. I had bitten my lips red and I was slumped over in my chair, drooping with disappointment. "I guess there's nothing I can do about it," I sighed to myself.

I didn't realize that those were the magic words.

Suddenly, my chair jumped forward of its own accord. *An earthquake?* But the moment the thought popped into my head my face slammed forward into my Chiloé-covered wall. Doused in pain, I knew who it was.

I tried to beat him to his punchline.

"You're about to say, 'are you awake now?' aren't you?" I rubbed my throbbing forehead.

I turned around and saw King standing there, wearing tattered, light brown clothes. He looked like a traveler. Maybe he wanted to go to Chiloé too.

"I'm showing up a lot this year," he said. "You've got a serious problem."

"What?"

"Remember when you gave up on the Colo-Colo stuff too? You were better off when you were a snot-nosed idiot elementary schooler who thought you were invincible."

I felt shocked. So that's what he thought of me when I was young. My relatives called me an angel from heaven.

King snorted at my thoughts and snatched my chair out from under me, sending me toppling to the floor. He sat down in the chair, folded his arms, and stared down at me on the floor. He seemed to enjoy looking down at me.

"I'll say it for your own good: you never get to change your name in life. Well, unless you take your spouse's name. But still, you'll live and die as a Kitazato."

Thanks, Captain Obvious.

"Keep that in mind in this situation. Your father will never stop being your father. Well, unless maybe your parents divorce. But your parents seem to get along fine, so there's nothing to worry about. Unless . . . no, never mind. I've gotten off track."

King cleared his throat.

"What I'm trying to ask is: Can you always live under the strict rules of your father? That's what you're dealing with now. You'll be following those rules this year, next year, and the next year. And you'll keep on dealing with him after that too. Strict parents are strict parents no matter what. So if you're just giving up now, you may as well do only what your parents permit you to do for the rest of your life. Is that good enough for you?"

I felt like a stuffed sandbag full of frustration as I lay there, trying to absorb King's straight talk. I was about to burst out tears of sand all over the place. I wanted to argue back, to deny it somehow, but I had no words.

I had never opposed my parents before, and this was the first time that I had even tried to convince them to let me do something. I tried to argue my case to them so many times. In the middle of it, I would sometimes catch a glimpse of my silent father, and it was honestly terrifying. Still, I tried. I made new printouts, new arguments to convince them. I kept struggling. Kept fighting. But every time, by the time I finished, they shook their heads "no." What else could I do?

I bit my chewed-out lips and tasted blood. Tears filled my eyes.

King kept staring at me. I tried to respond to him, but he wouldn't say anything more. We looked at one another. His big, straightforward, honest eyes stared back at me. When I looked into them, I knew that they wouldn't lie to me. He brought out the best in me every time we met. But this time I couldn't speak to him. Instead, tears pooled in my eyes and fell over my cheeks.

"Don't cry! What are you, a baby?"

I closed my eyes, expecting more than just words. But nothing came.

I opened my eyes.

King kept staring at me. He made a fist and poked me in the chest. I felt a pulse in my heart.

"Where's your determination?"

"Huh?"

"What you and Yuho are lacking is the fighting spirit," King said. "The determination to go to Chiloé, even if the whole world is against it. Of course, your parents are against it! It's two fourteen-year-old kids going to some South American island they've never even been to before! When you accept their rejection at face value, of course you won't be able to go. Your determination isn't getting through to your parents. The problem isn't your parents—it's your own lack of determination."

"Not enough . . . determination? No!" I protested. "We were determined, but it wasn't enough. It didn't work because it wasn't enough." I paused. "But I suppose that's no different from not having enough determination."

My chest was hot where King had touched me. He kept going, raining painful truth on me with his words.

"That's right! And even if they gave you permission, that wouldn't even solve half of your problems. You are taking this too lightly! You are being a spoiled little kid! Think about it. Think about who was going to buy the bicycles you were going to go to Chiloé on? You said you would sleep in a tent, but what about food? Are you expecting me to come and cook for you?"

King was getting riled up. His frankness was starting to irritate me. But every word he said was true.

"What about if you got sick on the trip? Would you have money to go to a doctor? Did you just think you parents would just let you go on the trip and hand over the cash? You can't just say 'I wanna travel!' That's the same as saying, 'I wanna travel, so can you arrange everything for me please?' You're babies, relying on your parents for every last thing. For babies like you it's a thousand years too early to take a trip by yourself."

I felt that a thousand years was a slight exaggeration, but he wasn't wrong. We expressed what we wanted to our parents, and we thought that if they gave us permission, we'd somehow just figure everything out. We figured that even if we ran out of money, we'd get by. Or, they'd just give us enough money and wish us a safe trip.

We were both dumb and spoiled. Quite a combination.

"It's not so simple to protect your ego," King said. "Up until now, you basically just threw a tantrum and got what you wanted. Hey—wittle baby! Wittle baby want a piece of candy?"

King sounded pretty weird doing baby talk.

"You've gotten everything you wanted with whining and arm wrestling. Those abilities won't be enough to defeat the next boss. Do you get it now? Up until now, the people around you accepted your pointless struggle. They helped you. Basically, your ego was a nuisance to others, so they caved in. After all, it wasn't a big deal to them."

Bull's-eye.

Even though in elementary school I was determined to master selfishness, I hadn't yet bothered to thoroughly investigate how to do that. All I had done was whine and demand, and eventually the other side caved in. Like King was saying—baby stuff.

My chest grew so hot that it felt like it was starting to cave in on itself.

"To live selfishly means that even if the whole world opposes you, even if no one else is willing to lend you a hand, you get what you want and satisfy your ego. It's not just getting them to say yes. You can't afford to wait for other people's permission.

The only one who can embrace your ego, protect it, and answer its prayers is you and you alone. If you lack determination, you may as well be missing your ego."

Determination.

Responsibility.

Yes, I had left things up to others. I was nothing more than a baby chick, clucking for permission, waiting for my parents to feed me what I wanted. I had been getting by on temporary measures.

I had to take responsibility for my life.

So how could I do that?

"I guess I'll have to teach you." King let out a sigh. "I can show you a trick."

"A trick?"

King twisted his neck. I could hear his bones snap.

Did he mean a magic trick?

A little question mark floated above my head. King's response knocked it straight into the sky.

"Don't give up on what your ego desires. Give up giving up. Now that's determination!"

His words blew my mind.

How can you give up giving up?

That's what determination is?!

If you negate a negative thing, it turns into a positive. There was that Noriyuki Makihara ballad that went, "I won't say that I definitely won't fall in love again." Is that what King meant?

That little floating question mark whipped back like a boomerang. My face had gone pale. But part of me felt like I could understand what he meant, so I didn't give up on that feeling. I thought hard, grinding my teeth.

"That's right. Think so hard about it that you throw up. Struggle, wriggle, squirm."

Instead of throwing up, I quickly got a pounding headache. But I didn't want to lose my precious determination. I had an instinctual feeling that this was incredibly important for me to understand in order to be my best self. If I gave up now, I wouldn't be me. I was thinking so hard my head felt like it was going to explode!

"I won't give up on my ego!" I shouted. "Even if the whole world opposes me! No matter what anyone says! If words don't work, I'll take action! I'll take action!"

I felt like someone had lit a fire inside me. Determination started to silently ignite within me.

The pounding in my head faded away. King put a hand on my head. His hand was big, heavy, and warm.

"Now *that's* determination," he said.

King ruffled my hair, just like my dad used to do. His hand

wasn't too different from my dad's. I calmed down and my whole body felt warm.

"Who are you, King?"

The question that was stuck inside me this whole time suddenly popped out.

His hand still on my head, King answered my question as if it were no big deal:

"You don't know yet? I'm *you*."

"Huh?"

"I'm the guy with the world's biggest ego. I'm you."

King knocked on my chest lightly. I glanced down at the spot where he had touched me.

"Listen up. Humans live a messy existence. Sometimes you're strong and sometimes you're weak. Sometimes you give it your all and sometimes you give up. Every person has so many different selves. We use our different selves to adapt to the environment around us—different parts of the world, like 'parents' or 'school' or 'society.' Even if you don't want to, you'll end up that way. Some people can't handle it and give up on living.

"Because you have so many different selves inside you, it feels messy and hard to decide what to do. But take it from me—all of those selves aren't worth shit.

"So there you are, all mixed up with the influences of different environments and emotions and common sense.

"I'm different. I'm your pure, selfish ego.

"I'm the original motive that has existed from the moment you were born. Want, desire, craving.

"The rules of society? Your environment? Common sense? Screw it all. I'm what you *really* want. I'm selfishness in practice, 0% contaminated, 100% pure. Your true self. Your purest, strongest self. I've controlled you at various times. That's why I call myself King—because that's what I am. Do you get it now?"

The most egotistical me is the strongest and truest version of me?

I thought that he came up with the name King just because he saw "The Naked King" written on the blackboard in school that day.

My true self? If he was me, how could his slaps hurt so much?

And can I really grow a beard like that?

And would I really be so harsh on myself?

Doubts and questions flooded my mind.

"I have so many questions," I started to say to King, but I didn't know where to begin.

Just like the ghost that appears before the hero at the start of his legendary journey, King had already vanished. I looked around my room but saw no one. Just the morning sun, shining through my window without a word.

It was already morning. I had never stayed up all night before, but I didn't feel tired in the slightest. Instead, I felt happy—like I had found a new beginning.

That day, Yuho and I put our heads together and discussed what was necessary to make our plan a reality. First, we made a list of what we needed: a bicycle, a tent, camping gear. Then we calculated the money necessary to buy those things, as well as food and other travel expenses.

Yuho and I turned over our rooms in search of all the cash we had, but it didn't match the sum we needed. Still, we weren't concerned. We had our determination. Of course, we weren't going to ask our parents—we'd set out to earn it. The only question was how.

Up until now, we had never made money on our own, just received an allowance.

Chile had more of an established black market than Japan. We had heard of plenty of kids earning money by doing some illegal thing or other, but they were criminals. Back in Japan, kids our age could just make money by taking some part-time job at a store, but we hadn't heard of any jobs that would take Japanese kids, at least in Santiago.

Facing this new monster of needing to find a job without any experience, we thought as hard as we possibly could. We thought and thought, squeezed the very dregs out of our thoughts, and eventually we got so hungry that we went into town to get something to eat.

We went to a mall that we frequented called Apumanque. While chewing on candy, we wandered through the mall and out to the open-air stores that surrounded the outside of the mall. These stalls were run by men who just sat around all day and smoked cigarettes. It didn't seem like anyone would say anything if we joined them.

So maybe we could sell something here, I thought. Yuho thought it was a good idea too, so we walked through the market and checked out every stall. Along the way, we saw one store that sold pendants made out of different coins from around the world. Then we realized that there were a bunch of other stores that also sold the same thing, each selling pendants out of whatever different coins they happened to have. And we didn't see any stores that sold pendants made out of Japanese yen coins.

That was it!

We high-fived. We didn't need to start up our own stall. We just needed to sell Japanese coins to the stalls that were already here!

I approached one of the shop owners and started asking him questions. When I asked him if he would buy Japanese yen coins from us, he told us he would, depending on the design. We had found a way!

The next day, I went around asking all of the Japanese kids at school and they gave me their spare yen coins. After class, Yuho and I brought the coins that we gathered to the shop owner.

It was my first business venture.

Starting out, I kept the more valuable 500-yen coins hidden. I only showed him the one-yen coins and began the negotiations.

At the time, the exchange ratio between the Japanese yen and the Chilean peso was roughly four to one. But he proposed a price much lower than that. So I decided to be daring and put a 100-yen coin down on the table. His offer for that was cheap too. He was trying to rip me off because I was just a kid, I figured. I decided to be even bolder and put the 500-yen down on the table and told him it was the most valuable Japanese coin out there. Which was true.

"This is 10,000 Japanese yen," I bluffed.

But the shop owner was a sly old geezer.

"It says 500 yen right here," he pointed. "And the exchange rate is printed right over there," he said, pointing across the mall to a money exchange. The exchange rate was clearly printed on the sign.

My first go was a strikeout. Yuho and I glanced at one another, but just then the shop owner spoke up.

"I can give you more for this one," he said, pointing at the five-yen coin.

"Why? The 500-yen coin is worth 100 times more than that one!" I shouted.

The shop owner laughed.

"What are you talking about? This five-yen coin is by far the coolest. The gold color is nice, and the fact that it's got a hole in it is really unique too."

He picked up the coin and put it to his eye, peeking through the hole at the sky.

What he said shocked me. I had assumed that the value of the coin was simply the value printed on it. So the higher the value, and the more I had, the more I'd get. Everyone knew that. But the shop owner didn't seem interested in the value written on the coin, but his own aesthetic sense. That's how he determined the coin's worth.

Amazing! So different people have different senses of value!

That first negotiation taught me a valuable lesson about business. Even if something didn't have value to me, it could have immense value to another person.

I heard a drumroll and victory music in my head. Yohei's "business" skills have leveled up!

The shop owner ended up buying all of the yen that I had gathered, concluding my first coin-business venture. I had ended up taking all of my friend's leftover coins, so after that deal I didn't have anything else to sell him.

It was time for me to try my hand at my next business. We decided to start our own English-conversation school.

In Santiago, there was a Japanese school. All the classes were in Japanese, and of course they spoke Japanese in their daily lives; it was a school totally built for Japanese people. And even though some of them could speak Spanish, almost nobody in that school spoke English.

Yuho and I went to an international school, so we could choose for our classes to be in English or Spanish. Since I had chosen English classes, I didn't have any problem speaking, but compared to native speakers at my school, my English was pretty shit. Still, I figured my shit English would be useful for other Japanese people that couldn't even speak a lick of English. I remembered the lesson about value that I learned from my coin business, and immediately started to get to work.

First, targeting students at the Japanese school, we started our "Weekend English Conversation School" recruitment program. Fortunately, Yuho's mom, who was a part of the more moderate faction that nevertheless ultimately rejected the presentation we made at the camping trip, decided to help us out. She reached out to other parents whose kids went to the Japanese school. As a mother of five, she had plenty of connections, and talked to pretty much every mom at the Japanese elementary school. As a result, we ended up with even more students than we were expecting.

In my mind, I pumped my fist hard. *You're quite the businessman, Yohei!*

As a beginner businessman, that was the moment when I started to sense that I could actually do it. So we took our shit English, claimed it was proficient and authentic, and started our school with smiles on our faces.

All of our students were elementary schoolers who had never learned English before. From the perspective of their parents, it would be valuable if we could teach the kids even something that sounded remotely like English. And since we were watching the kids after school, that was a secondary valuable service. We were like babysitters who helped the kids do some of their homework. While we looked after the kids, the parents would go shopping or golfing. The word about our English school spread.

And for the students, our classes pretty much consisted of just talking and messing around, which they seemed to enjoy. After class, we would all play soccer or basketball. Parents and kids alike were happy. We had managed to give both groups something that they felt was valuable. The only thing that slipped through the cracks was actually improving their English skills. Still, Yuho and I were over the moon. Soon enough, we had saved enough money to actually go on our trip.

We were nearly as surprised as our parents. So they convened a new grand assembly meeting between the four of them.

By this point, our parents had one concern: that if they didn't give us permission, we might do something reckless out of sheer dissatisfaction. In other words, since we already had the money, we might just set out on our journey whenever we wanted. They didn't have the safeguard of us being unable to travel since we had to rely on them for money.

Their conclusion was: that being the case, if we went, we had to promise to them not to do anything dangerous or reckless.

Grand assembly concluded!

At long last, by our own efforts, we won their permission. We did it with our own discipline, our own hard work, our own determination.

A few months had passed since we'd decided to go on our trip.

Many preparations were made; tears were shed. But now that we had beaten our parents, we had a new adventure coming our way, an ultimate battle that had the potential to truly level up our egos.

It all felt like it happened so quickly after our parents gave us permission. With the money we saved, and according to our plans, we purchased the GT mountain bikes we had long wanted. We spent hours brushing up on the details of our plan with our parents. Their colleagues even held us a surprise celebration in honor of our journey, and we received countless words of support. Our expectations sky-high and our hearts full, we at last embarked on our legendary journey.

Our epic adventure to Chiloé, a mysterious island 800 miles away, began. But it didn't go as planned; not in the slightest. It would take me a whole other book to write out all the details, so I'll save that for another day.

However, to summarize it in a few bullet points, this is more or less how it went:

- We went broke way faster than expected.
- Every time we traveled between villages in Chiloé, we quickly ran out of water, and experienced mirages and illusions like parched desert wanderers. Often, we barely made it to the oasis—the next village.
- Unable to abate our hunger, we snuck aboard a fishing boat and were caught trying to steal fish.
- In a village we passed, we participated in a Guinness World Record with the rest of the village. We helped prepare a one-ton salmon for consumption and ate it all in one day.
- We were pursued, at various times, by police and priests.
- Plenty of times we slept on the road, as well as in strangers' houses.
- At the start, there was so much going on every day and I was so excited that I got a nosebleed. Sometimes my nose bled so badly that we had to pull over and take a rest.

We experienced failure countless times, but that's simply bound to happen on a journey as epic as ours.

One of the legends that we read about was the forest-dwelling dwarf of the forests of Chiloé, the Trauco. According to the legends, the Trauco lures maidens with a sweet scent and has sex with them.

The erotic elements of the Chiloé legends had played a major part in inspiring my fourteen-year old mind to want to go there. I'd also wanted La Viuda, the black-clothed widow, to embrace me from behind, but the "sex" tales of the Trauco inspired me more. Yuho admitted to me one night that he felt the same way. So it turned out that both of us had embarked on a legendary journey in part for the sake of teenage horniness.

But it turned out that we were the ones being lured in by the sweet scent of the Trauco all along. The mystery of Chiloé drew us in and forced us to experience a lot for the first time. Now I'm sure of it—the legends of Chiloé are true, every last one of them.

This legendary journey was a huge event in my life, but in Chile, every day shocked me in its own way. Soccer, parties, mischief . . .. Besides the legendary journey, I experienced countless other, smaller adventures. I made countless memories. I had more fun than I'd ever had before, and precisely for that reason, it all ended in the blink of an eye.

In Chile, I had developed my intuition and my selfishness.

I was confident that I could protect my ego in any situation. So with those new tools and my new self-confidence, I returned to Japan.

I had no way of expecting that when I returned to Japan, I'd be facing a new and more fearsome obstacle than ever before.

Chapter Five
FLIP THE SWITCH

A very fast four years had gone by since I moved to Chile. It was spring. I was trying to enjoy every day to the fullest up until my junior high school graduation, which was coming up in June. My friends back in Japan had already graduated in March, and most had taken their high school entrance exams and started at different high schools.

Since Nido de Aguilas was an integrated school that included all grades K–12, I didn't have to take a high school entrance exam. So I didn't get swept up in all of the studying and fierce competition. I didn't get the sense from the high school students around me that they were particularly concerned about getting into college, either.

In Chile, it's easy to get into college, but hard work to graduate—the exact opposite of the way things are in Japan. So even seniors didn't have to worry too much about college entrance exams. Swept up in the carefree attitude of my fellow classmates, I spent all of my days enjoying myself, not worrying about studying in the slightest.

Since our family had lived abroad for a long time, my father's company had a system that allowed us all to come back to Japan for a short period. I suppose the company wanted us to come back and breathe the Japanese the air from time to time.

So with my graduation in June coming up, we took a trip back to Japan.

Right after we arrived in our hometown of Saitama, I took off and went straight to Shibuya. At the time, it was one of the hippest neighborhoods in Tokyo. I was in search of some thrills. During my time in Chile, I read about Shibuya in Japanese magazines I could occasionally get my hands on. Sometimes I saw it in Japanese TV programs that we had on videocassette. I always thought it seemed like a fascinating place. Shibuya and Saitama aren't that far apart, but before I came to Chile I had still been in elementary school, so there was never any reason to go to Shibuya.

I kept wondering what it would be like as I got on the train with my childhood friend. We took the short train ride and got off at Shibuya Station. The second I stepped outside I was completely overwhelmed.

At the time, Shibuya was at the height of its status as a center of youth culture and fashion. Day and night, the Shibuya Center-Gai shopping street was flooded with all types of people you couldn't even imagine back in Chile, like the *ganguro-kogyaru*, who were fashion-obsessed teenage girls with bleached hair, ridiculously dark-tanned skin, and faces smeared with colorful make-up. Or like the gangs of teenage delinquents that roamed the city in groups in tough black leather or sagging jeans and heavy sweatshirts. Down back alleys, tough-looking Iranians and Israelis were peddling everything from semi-shady coun-terfeit prepaid phone cards to all-out illegal drugs. When I took a close look at one of my childhood friends, I realized that she was a bit of a *ganguro-kogyaru* herself.

A few days later, we went to a jam-packed, flashy Shibuya club. Guys and girls, wearing whatever clothes they thought were in style, chased after each other flirting, drinking, and dancing madly in the deafening music.

Shibuya's passionate, dazzling atmosphere had me spell-bound.

In Santiago, there was no entertainment district like Shibuya or Shinjuku in Tokyo. There was a red light district full of strip clubs and brothels, but that was it. Certainly there was no place that a middle-schooler could go even if he wanted to.

Since there were a lot of rich kids at Nido de Aguilas, students would often have parties at their big houses with music and drinking. Those parties were fun, but since they only invited their friends, it was boring to see the same people over and over again. Chile also had disco clubs, but they were a world apart from Shibuya's packed clubs. In terms of the size of the crowds, the volume of the music, and the appetite of the partygoers, Shibuya won on all counts.

These parties were just for young people, and they felt to-tally wild, even to the young people in attendance. There were so many different people from all over that, even if you went two days in a row, you had very little chance of meeting the same person twice.

Everything was new and exciting.

Shibuya also had a remarkable number of high school students roaming around at the time. Bleached hair. Saggy pants. Miniskirts. High, baggy socks. Excited to wear anything but their school uniforms, high school students paraded about Center-Gai Street like they owned the place.

It wasn't all fun. Shibuya had all sorts of dangers that didn't exist back in Chile. Gangs of teenagers in turf wars, robbing salarymen and even attacking people who were wearing Nike Air Max sneakers to get the prized Jordan brand shoes. Everywhere you went was a whirlpool of enthusiasm, spitting out new cultures and trends on every block, both good and bad. The more we explored Shibuya, the more I found myself astonished that there could be *this* many young people just like myself, and that they could be having *that* much fun. I vowed in that moment to never become an adult without having experienced this kind of fun.

I realized that I wanted to live in Japan.

I felt a sort of courage inside me that I had never experienced back in Chile. As soon as we got back to Chile, I had an honest conversation with my parents. I wanted to go to high school in Japan. I could get a better education in Japan, for one, and as a native Japanese person, I wanted to grow into an adult with a firm understanding of Japanese culture. I passionately made my case. Of course, when I referred to "Japanese culture" I was thinking about the culture of Shibuya, but referring to it as "Japanese culture" in the general sense would resonate more with my parents.

My parents had always supported my education and sincerely wanted me to study more. The "cherry-on-top" was that I said I wanted to experience Japanese culture. That made it easy for them. They agreed.

As soon as I graduated from Nido de Aguilas Middle School (along with everyone else), and along with my older sister, who had just graduated high school and was off to take Japanese university entrance exams, I found myself on a plane back to Narita Airport.

I lived in Saitama with my grandparents for a while. I came back to Japan in June and planned to start high school in September. So I studied for the entrance examinations in July and August.

It wasn't nearly enough time. But at least I could experience life back in Japan for the first time in ages. I met up with old friends, lost myself in reading manga, and recharged my batteries for a new school and new life.

As for studying, I figured I'd be fine without it. I was a genius, after all.

It was that baseless confidence I carried ever since elementary school. I calculated that if everyone around me was giving

100% effort, I could get away with 10%. *That* was my actual thought.

Sure, I had failed tests before, but in elementary school I had more or less gotten by. Even if I didn't listen in class, I could usually figure out the answers. (Genius level: 100.)

In Chile, before my English got up to speed, my grades were pretty awful. But I always assumed that once my English got better, I'd be able to keep up. And that turned out to be the case. My grades improved. (Genius level: 120.)

Math class gave me particular confidence. Because of differences in the curriculum, Chile was way behind Japan in math. Even in the first year of middle school, knowing addition and subtraction was enough. So as a kid who could do multiplication and division, I was basically treated as a genius. (Genius level: 350!)

Yep. According to me, I was still the genius I had always been.

Without putting any effort into studying, I had managed to get by even in English class out of sheer, on-the-spot intuition. There was no way anything could go wrong.

But then my entrance exam results came in. I was utterly annihilated.

(Genius level: 0.)

I learned at last that I couldn't hold a candle to the Japanese standard. I'm sure my parents knew what they were doing.

They knew they were shoving me off into the abyss by sending me back to contend with the beast that is Japanese entrance examinations.

I was so underprepared that when Japanese kanji appeared on the exam, I wondered to myself why Chinese characters were showing up. I supposed it was some sort of Chinese test. And as for math, the source of my boundless self-confidence, I couldn't even understand the questions.

My top choices, the most popular schools, even the back-ups to my back-ups—my genius slipped and stumbled, and I couldn't get into a single one. But there was no way I was going back to Chile. I had to get into high school in Japan—literally anywhere would do! At least I had my determination.

I gave up on getting into good schools. I gave up on my dream schools. I consulted my network of friends and family and arrived at a conclusion: If I sent a letter appealing my case, there might be a school that would let me in even without having passed the exam. I heard rumors about something like that at a private all-boy's boarding school in Chiba prefecture.

It worked. Even though I had longed to spend time in Shibuya, I ended up going to a remote school in Chiba, buried deep in the mountains. I ended up giving up quite a lot, and I wasn't exactly happy about it. But I wanted to go to a Japanese high school, no matter where. If I could just go, I would be able to enjoy that idyllic, rosy student life, after all. I swelled with anticipation.

But my student life ended up being more charcoal than rose-colored.

It was the fall of my first year. I, an innocent, cheery transfer student, encountered a new enemy. It was two words that I had never thought about in my life: *University exams.*

All of my fellow students were already nose-deep in studying for them. All day at school it was study-time around the clock, even though everyone had more than two years left! Classes had turned entirely into preparation for university exams.

All the students believed that anyone who wanted to mess around and have fun had no future. Getting into a good university meant the world to them. They all tried to force that mindset onto me. I couldn't believe it.

There weren't many of them, but there were also some juvenile-delinquent types at my school. "Who gives a shit about college!" they spat.

But as soon as I started to agree with them, they looked over at me with contempt.

"Don't even think about hanging out with us!" they snarled.

I had plenty of experience dealing with these types from all of my arm wrestling and fighting back in Chile. But since the zeal of studying completely controlled the school's atmosphere, even the delinquents eventually started to catch on and study. I was left flexing and prepping for arm wrestling with myself and fights with nobody. I couldn't keep up in the entrance exams race, and I had no interest in doing so either.

Looking back on it, I think that most Japanese people use studying, part-time jobs, college, and eventually company employment as an excuse to give up on their real hopes and dreams. To put it another way, Japanese people live their lives giving up over and over again. Their lives are giant exercises in giving up.

I've never thought that way before, but when I was surrounded by the fierce effort of my classmates to study, I got the sense that I was on my way to giving up on my dream of a glorious high school life. Back in Chile, this would've been a nightmare scenario.

In Japan, I also saw bullying the likes of which I had never seen or even heard about in Chile, especially when it came to upperclassmen bullying underclassmen. Because it was a boarding school, there was plenty of time to bully outside of class. It happened to me too, but it didn't bother me. The isolation and friction I had experienced as a foreigner during my time in Chile was far more painful and malicious. The more pressing issue was what to do about college entrance exams, or whether I could even pass them in the first place. Stress accumulated fast.

My high school exams had proved that my academic ability was painfully insufficient. I was at the bottom of the bottom of the bottom of the bottom of my class. I had spent three years in Chile acing classes simply by knowing the gist of things. Aside from my English, which would come in handy for college entrance exams, I knew absolutely none of the material. In fact, I lacked every imaginable piece of the essential foundation for the material, which was normally built up in Japan through three hardworking years of middle school. And I still had no intentions of giving up my youth.

I hated the oppressive atmosphere that all of my entrance exam–obsessed classmates created. To make matters worse, I had no interest in the content or material that they were all studying, either.

Let's say just for argument's sake that, even though I didn't have the remotest speck of interest in becoming a scientist, I memorized the entire periodic table, top to bottom. What would I even get out of that? I needed someone to explain that to me! If I was going to memorize things, at least teach me how to use a condom or how to survive with my bare hands in the Amazon rainforest. In Japan, they'd just say that there weren't teachers for that, but there were at Nido de Aguilas! Over in Chile, I learned so many basic, fundamental life lessons from my teachers, for one, but also from my friends. None of that knowledge would be of any use for examinations. Rather, having all of that life knowledge was turning out to be a serious handicap.

Still, I didn't want to go so far as to give up on studying

altogether and completely bask in the glory of youth. It's not that I didn't want to go to a good college—I did. I just had other things I wanted to do as well.

I figured that people who got into Tokyo or Kyoto University believed in something more important than grades and good schools. It would be incredibly cool to get top grades, get into a top school, get a job at a top company, and still proclaim that good grades and good schools were all bullshit. But it was totally lame to whine and complain about the system if you were a failure, like me, who couldn't even choose his own high school. A whimpering puppy. Rejecting the system and running away was the easy route.

I had decided to live in Japan. And in Japan, your educational background can set the course of your life. At least that's what I thought at the time. Perhaps what my parents and teachers kept saying had finally gotten to my head.

Of course, I felt confident that I could have a great life even if I didn't go to college. But I was concerned about being labeled an outcast that drifted off from society. I wasn't worried that it might stop me from achieving my dreams, but I wanted to be able to show everyone that I could do just as well at their own game, and beat them. I also got the vague sense that no matter what happened now, someday I could finally break free of it all.

However. *However.* To start, I—who had no ambition or

determination besides protecting my own ego—had never even had the remotest thought or vision of what I wanted to do in the future. On top of that, it was terrifying to even think about how much studying I would need to do in order to catch up and succeed on college entrance exams. Given the amount of time I spent messing around in middle school, I calculated my development had been delayed, at minimum, by three years. So even if I studied a normal amount for three years, that would put me at about the level of a first-year high school student. I would have to resolve to be a *ronin*—a wandering, masterless samurai—AKA the high school student who has to study an extra year to get into college. Even though I wanted to enjoy my youth starting *today,* I needed four or five years of nonstop studying. I wouldn't be able to experience anything. I'd have to resort to cram school in order to avoid becoming a ronin.

And until I could catch up, just how many dreams would I have to give up on?

I want to party nonstop and bask in the glory of my youth.
I want to get into a good college.
They were both simple motivations. Two selfish motivations that directly contradicted each other. And I didn't have the slightest idea of how to do both of them at the same time.

I looked around my room, a small dormitory room in the

Chiba mountains. I threw myself onto the bed. I had the bottom half of a small bunk bed in a small room. The room was as bleak as a prison cell. As a first-year, the rooms had four beds each. Then, as a second-year, two beds per room, and finally as a third-year, you had the room to yourself. There was also a middle school dormitory on the same lot with about forty kids to a room. So I supposed I was living in luxury compared to that.

I stared up at the dark, flat underside of the bed above me. The other kid wasn't there. I had to do it now.

"You're there, aren't you?" I said.

I'm *you*, King had told me. I could still remember the feeling when he had touched my chest. King was my pure, selfish will. So that meant that when I was talking with King before, I had really been talking to myself. I had been talking to myself and also whacking myself. No wonder the kids on the bus had been so surprised.

Meeting King really meant facing myself. King hadn't shown up since he told me that. Because I understood that, even if it hadn't been perfect, I had been able to live as my true self.

But this time I needed him. My two separate desires were clashing against each other. It was like having two Kings, opposing one another. Two wills, two Kings.

If I searched deep within myself, surely I'd be able to find him. But even though I had called out to him for the first time, no answer came.

No, he must be there, I thought to myself, looking around the room. But he wasn't.

Had he left me behind?

Suddenly anxious, I jumped out of bed, unable to believe it. Then I gripped the side of the upper bunk and pulled myself up to take a look.

King was lying down on the bed with his back to me, reading a manga. He was reading *Slam Dunk*, a basketball manga. It was one of my favorites. The upperclassman shooting guard Mitsui was giving an inspirational speech. Was it just me or did King's eyes look a little teary? I stopped myself before saying it out loud, for fear of vicious retribution.

"If you've been there the whole time, say something," I grumbled, pulling myself up onto the bunk.

King didn't even turn around. Maybe he really was crying. But when he spoke, his voice was far colder than Mitsui's.

"Don't talk to me," he said. "I'm not your teacher or your parent. So you want to get into a good college? Don't ask me. That's not my area of expertise. You're the one who fucked up your exams. If you want to get into a good college, work yourself to the bone if that's what it takes. But don't ask me."

Somehow, I understood what he meant.

I wanted to be one of the cool people who got into a great

university and then insisted that education doesn't matter. But studying wasn't my style. I could hardly get myself to sit at my desk. So even if my true intention was to get into a good college, I had to face the reality that I had no desire to study.

I had chosen the wrong person to consult, apparently.

But King was the only person there for me. I had been waiting for him to come back again. He let out a putrid fart.

What could he have possibly been eating to make such a disgusting smell?

I turned around for a second to relieve myself of the stink, thought for a moment, and spoke to his back.

"King. You can ignore me if you want. But in the end, you don't really have a choice. Until you face me, we won't be able to solve this problem. Anything I decide to do without your input will only be like living a lie. You don't want that, do you?"

"I don't want anything at all," King retorted, glancing back at me.

When I caught a glimpse of the corner of his eye, I saw that there weren't any tears, just plain old, crusty eye mucus. Had he been asleep in the top bunk?

"You know who I am now, don't you?" King asked. "So if you ignore my advice, no matter how hard I try to convince you, it won't even matter. That's what I mean when I say I don't want anything at all. If you ignore what you really want and focus on studying, you'll lose your three years of high school doing something you hate. And even after all that, you might still fail your exams. Or, you'll reluctantly go to university. Or you'll keep lying to yourself for another year or two as a ronin. That's what you get for ignoring me. You might be better off that way. Okay, good night."

King farted even louder than before and rolled over in bed.

So he was sleeping! I thought. *And holy hell, that smell! I thought that the smell and volume of farts had an inverse relationship! No, I don't have time to be thinking about this!*

Up until now, whenever I had given up on something, King would appear on his own and help me. For the first time, even though I had asked for his help, he turned his back and farted at me. What did he mean by lying to myself? This was a whole new level for him. Unable to bear the smell anymore, I was about to give up and drop back down to the lower bunk. I had just wanted to talk things through with him, but it turned out to be pointless.

"But still—"

As soon as I started to speak, I felt a blow to my face. He had slapped me with the back of his hand, sending me falling down from the upper bunk.

Every time we met, at the very least, his fighting skills were upgraded.

I crashed on the floor flat on my back, gazing straight at the ceiling. I couldn't move at all, like a turtle flipped on its shell. King peered out over the edge of the bunk and stared down at me. How many times had he looked down at me now? Suddenly, King's previously sleepy eyes flashed open, like a monster awakening from the dead. The piercing gaze reminded me of the terrifying coach from *Slam Dunk*, Mr. Anzai—also known as the White Haired Devil.

"But still, but still? But *what?* Some new excuse that you've come up with? Don't make me listen to your childish bullshit. To a stupid moronic crybaby try-hard fool like you, maybe what your parents think, or your social position in school, matters that much to you. Is that why you're making all these excuses? And what next? Did you think this would make me happy? Why do you think I've helped you out all these years? For you to throw it all away? I can't keep saving your ass forever!"

King flung the manga down at me. I plucked it off and glimpsed a speech-bubble coming from Mr. Anzai: "If you give up now . . ."

King let out a big sigh. The rage in his swollen face slowly drained away. His eyes even lost their strength, their dark color fading. King, no matter how much I disliked him, had always been on my side. But his eyes had turned cold. I sensed that he was ready to give up on me. And if King gave up, it was all over for me. Game, set, match. Not just that—this was more than a game. I might never be able to find what I really wanted ever again!

"Please!" I leapt up and pleaded to King with all of my heart. "Tomorrow! I'll prove it to you by tomorrow! I know that you don't believe in school. But I'll convince you otherwise— just give me one day! I'll protect our ego! So just wait one day for me, please!"

King's face turned paler and paler.

"Please this, please that. What do you want from me?" It wasn't King's usual strong voice, brimming with confidence. Confusion, weakness, even kindness had slipped into his husky voice. I felt a chill across my body. At this rate, King might vanish altogether. Things were looking bad.

"Wait a second!"

King looked at me with a resigned expression.

"All right, I'll wait twenty-four hours, no more, no less."

He spoke calmly, as if to soothe me.

"Just make sure you come up with answer in time that's so inspiring it makes my heart skip a beat," he said. "I've always been the one to cheer you up. Now do the same for me. If you manage to convince me about school and what's best for your future, I think we can say that you've officially flipped the switch."

Switch? What switch?

"Once you flip the switch, you'll understand. Because your world will never be the same."

King disappeared as soon as he said the words.

My room suddenly felt huge, like an immense cavern.

I couldn't sleep that night.

King and I spoke at midnight. That gave me until midnight the next day. I couldn't afford to waste even a second.

I played sick to get out of class and sat down at my desk in my room until night. When I couldn't make any progress, I did pushups to get my blood flowing. I had to convince him . . . no, I had to inspire him and make his heart skip a beat. How could I possibly convince someone of the value of school when they hate school as much as King?

Oh?

My push-up count was over 200. I couldn't think straight from the fatigue.

I felt a click, like I had suddenly made progress. That's right—I had to start by boiling things down to the simplest possible answer. I had to get rid of all of the excess. I had to find the simplest me.

And what was the simplest me?

Overconfident. A self-declared genius. A kid that can achieve anything he sets his mind to. Someone who couldn't stop fooling around or resist worldly temptations.

So I thought, *The simplest possible me hates the things he hates. He's easy to flatter. He does what it takes. He's a bit of an idiot too. But that's the honest truth. He's King.*

But on the other hand, he's also the one who cares about pride and what his parents think of him, one who takes exams even if he doesn't want to, one who hates the notion of giving up, so he makes excuses for himself. That's all I was right then. The dregs of me.

I had to gather up the dregs and throw them away. I tried to think about it from King's perspective. First, I needed to make what I have to do very clear. Of course, I had to study my ass off, but more than that, I needed to calculate exactly how many hours it would take.

Assuming that a student who gets into a top school studies hard for about seven hours per day on average, that meant 2,555 hours of studying per year. Over three years that made 7,665 hours. Great. Let's forget about the three years of middle school I had missed out on. The assumption was that if I study enough to get by in high school, I'd naturally be able to catch up on middle school along the way. Regardless, I had to figure out how I'd be able to study for 7,665 hours.

By this point I had done more than 400 pushups. My chest hurt. *Let's stop. Let's give up,* but at that moment, something flashed in my mind.

How about a plan that gets it all done in just six months?

I had six months left in my first year of high school. In a mere six months, I'd master everything necessary to pass college entrance exams and get into a top school.

I hyped myself up about it. I could do it. Then the fun

could come afterward. I'd bask in the glory of my youth in hip Shibuya and nearly kill myself from partying too much. Six months of studying for two years of playing. That would be enough to convince King!

It would be 7,665 hours in six months. No problem! That only meant . . . forty-two hours per day.

So we were over twenty-four hours.

If I studied for eight hours a day for a half-year, I'd only hit 1,460 hours of studying. Not even close to enough. No! I What was going on? There had to be a way!

I hit 500 pushups (at least in my heart's approximate count). I had almost no power left. Speaking of which, working out is all about the number of reps you do. Every rep was equally important.

That's it!

I had to lift more weight per rep—concentrate and study harder than the average Joe. No, I had to concentrate five times harder than any high school student at the top of the class! If I did that, I could multiply the number of total hours I studied by five. So 1,460 times five made 7,300 hours in just six months of studying! It was about 400 hours short, but I figured my genius flair could carry me the rest of the way.

Of course, there were some kids out there that studied eight hours per day, but none of them had concentration abilities five times stronger than average. And since both King and

I knew that I was a genius, I was sure he wouldn't have any complaints about those leftover 400 hours. But most of all, I was sure he'd see the appeal in getting all my studying done in a half year to have two years of nonstop partying.

I looked at my watch. It was 11:50 PM. Just in time!

With all my strength, I heaved myself up to the top bunk, dragging my ass over the top.

King was sitting cross-legged on the bed. I was dripping with sweat from all the pushups and grinning from ear to ear with my new idea. He didn't look any paler than he did yesterday, and had a strong, stern expression. Even before I had said a word, I could tell that King knew everything. He spoke in a soft voice.

"Are you really going to do this?"

I nodded.

"How are you going to concentrate five times harder than a top student?"

"That's part of the deal," I said, following the plan I had rehearsed in my head. "To you, the most important thing is for me to enjoy my youth. But at this rate, everything is just a half-measure—I can't properly study or enjoy myself. So if you can teach me a special concentration method, I'll be able to study all I need in just six months. And then, starting six months from now, I'll go all out. No matter how mad my teachers get, I'll go crazy with partying.

"So please teach me! You're a genius, aren't you? Teach me your ways! Tell me how to follow in your footsteps! No, how to chase after you—and maybe even win!"

There was a long silence.

It was true that if I flattered King, he might get on board more easily. But it wasn't my intention to flatter. It was how I really felt. I had no doubt that King was an amazing person. He had never been wrong about me, my feelings, or what I ought to do.

King slowly nodded.

"Got it. I'm on board."

All of the sudden, I felt my pores open. Every hair on my body stood at attention and shivered in a burst of wind. This was King's determination! Determination so strong that another person can feel it—determination strong enough to change the world. This was going to become a six months unlike any other in my life. I just knew it.

Chapter Six
HYPER-FOCUS: MY OWN WORLD

"You've chosen to die on this hill," King said. "If you fail, despite my help here, it's going to be all over for you. If you can't succeed—no, if you don't succeed—which you want to do from the very bottom of your heart—then you'll be less than a man. You may as well be dead. Effort is important, and so is having a plan, but none of it matters more than simply getting into a top-class school. You'll need to just do it. Passing or failing, acceptance or rejection, none of it matters, because there's only one possible outcome. If you fail, you'll be a loser for the rest of your life. And I won't ever come back again. Is that okay with you?"

Even though King was talking about how he might disappear for good, I was grateful that he set it straight.

"I'll do it," I said, feeling determination flood every crevice of my body.

"All right, so go sit down at your desk," King said.

I jumped down from the upper bunk and sat at my desk. There was no turning back now.

"Open up your reference book."

"What?"

"The reference book. The course materials reference book."

I paused. "I haven't bought it yet."

"Are you kidding me?"

"Well, I just decided to study yesterday, so I wouldn't have even had time to buy it yet! I was trying to stop you from disappearing!"

"You shouldn't be the one angry in this situation."

"You promised to teach me! A man keeps his word!"

"Then go buy the reference book and get back here! That book has everything you need to get into a great school!"

"It's past midnight!" I exclaimed. "I can't buy one anywhere!"

"Then go the fuck to sleep!" King shouted.

"I'm sleeping!" I roared, climbing into bed. "I'm going the fuck to sleep!"

Totally exhausted, I passed out until noon the next day. King woke me up with a knee-drop to the chest.

I went straight to the bookstore and used every last yen I had to buy reference books. The books were as heavy as a human being and cost as much as the Imperial Palace. I lugged them back to my building and staggered into my dorm. I should've brought a cart to wheel them.

I dumped the reference books by the side of my desk. I stacked the first five books or so on top of my desk along with three mechanical pencils, three erasers, and two red pens. I lined up the various notebooks I bought and stared at the arrangement on my desk proudly. I sat up straight in the chair, feeling prepared to study, no matter what it took.

King stood silent for a moment, and then shoved everything off of my desk with a swoop of his arm.

"What are you doing?" I cried.

King had a stern glare. He didn't appear to be joking.

"Don't put anything that you don't need immediately on your desk," he said. "You need to use as little as possible at one time. One book, one pen, one eraser. If you don't need it, don't use it. What's on your desk should be everything. Place your things in the same place and formation every time. Every single time. Keep things consistent. Whenever you bring something unnecessary into the equation, it introduces a distraction. Eliminate distractions. Make your setup a complete habit."

I swallowed. "Got it."

King, who usually felt like a close family member or friend, had adopted an extraordinary strictness. I could feel tension in the air. It was the same feeling as when my dad got really mad. I didn't open my mouth if it wasn't absolutely necessary. I could hear the ticking on the clock loud and clear.

"The tension that you're feeling right now—that's important. You need it. If you're trying to memorize something, you need to be thinking that if you forget it, you'll die."

"If I forget it, I die," I repeated.

Okay, this was even more intense than when Dad got angry.

"You're not just going for something mediocre here. You say you can concentrate five times harder than any other student. Okay—so that means that if your rivals can remember a kanji after writing it fifteen times, then you have to remember it after writing it just three times. Every rep matters.

"The first time, grasp the character you're writing.

"The second time, remember it.

"The third time, carve it into your memory with a bloody knife.

"If you can't remember it after the third time, that's a strikeout. No exceptions. No practice. You're going straight to the show."

My stomach curdled. I felt cold sweat on the back of my neck. Tension threaded the air. Victory at all costs. I couldn't run. I wouldn't. I had to do it.

So I placed one pencil, one eraser, and one reference book on my desk, carefully arranging them. Until my studying concluded, I would maintain that same exact placement.

"Great," King said. "Now I'll show you how to get into that world."

"That world?" What the hell was he talking about?

Was I dreaming?

"This is real life," King said with a sigh. "Me, you, everything around us. All real."

King put his hands on my shoulders and whispered into my ear, like "that world" was a dire secret.

"From now own, you need to make a world of your own. A world as deep and silent as the sea. You need to immerse yourself in that world.

"Don't breathe. Forget it. Forget hunger, hot and cold, everything that matters in the world around you—drown it all. All those things will send you back to reality. You need to go deep in a different world, a world of your own. A world where nobody—nothing—can disturb you. Like a diver, swim across it in a single breath. Do you understand?"

"A world of my own," I said, nodding.

"Yes. You need to be completely immersed in your textbooks, in the problems. You need to precisely take in every word of every question, memorize them, understand them, and move to the next. Swim on until you can't hold in your breath any longer. At first you might not be able to hold it for long. But as you practice, you'll get better. If you don't, you won't make it in time. You need to be able to swim for eight hours straight, no breaks. Believe that you can do it."

What would it be like to swim in another world? As usual, I felt like I could just barely grasp the meaning of King's strange way of speaking. I realized that he was talking about something similar to when Yuho and I were roaming around Chiloé. The island had no streetlamps, so we had to make it to the next village before the sun set at all costs. Our water bottles were empty, our stomachs screaming for food, our bodies utterly exhausted.

We were hallucinating from thirst. Back then, in spite of it all, we kept going, forcing our flesh and bodies to keep on moving, dragging our pain and our thoughts out of the way. We kept pushing the bike pedals, kept moving forward. Our minds, not our bodies, were pushing the bike pedals. I realized that the legendary journey wasn't just for kicks, after all.

I looked up at King.

King was already staring back at me. His gaze bore deeply into mine, like he already knew what I wanted to tell him. He wouldn't look away. That made me happy.

"So, shall we get started?"

"Already?"

"In order to dive into the depths of your world, we need a ceremony. Silence. One minute of silence. In that minute, shake off all the distractions of reality."

"Okay, sure."

"Take deep breaths for one minute, and then open your eyes. Starting in that moment, you will be in your own world. You'll be immersed in letters, numbers, graphics, words, questions. Then you start swimming. Keep swimming. Swim until you can't anymore. Don't even think about coming back. Don't allow yourself to do anything else. There is no room for failure. Because if you do, that means you're dead." King took a breath. "Are you ready?"

King knew my answer, and he wasn't waiting for me to give it. I closed my eyes and fell into silence. I had to dive deep into a world without distractions.

The world that King was talking about—it turns out it really did exist.

At first it was painful. But I knew that if I gave up, it was all over. I focused so hard I got sick. But when I fully submerged into that world, everything began to change. As if the air had become precisely aligned with my body temperature, I could no longer feel cold or hot. While I could see the clock ticking out of the corner in my eye, as if in slow motion, there was no other sound or smell. In that world, I finally began to solve the study questions.

My own pace surprised me, to the point where I wasn't sure if the textbooks I bought would be enough. Of course, the fear that death would come the moment my attention broke kept me glued to the books. But eventually I began to even forget that fear, falling deep into my own world. In a way, I was free there.

After six months, I finished my studying.

An unexpected result followed.

When I had entered school, my academic abilities were at the lowest possible level. Six months later, I ended up getting one of the top one hundred scores out of all of the high schoolers in Japan on a university entrance mock exam, almost enough to get my name on TV. I was offered a spot at one of the top three cram schools in the country, an invitation-only school. I could've taken whatever course level I wanted for free for the rest of high school.

As if I'd ever go to cram school! I intended to keep my promise to King.

Once I concluded studying all three years' worth of material in six months, I quickly put everything aside, and resolutely tossed my reference books into the garbage. It was time to bask in the glory of my youth for my two remaining years of high school and party so hard that I almost died. First things first—I had to get to Shibuya.

I left a note in my dorm that read "I won't be back for a while," and proceeded to play hooky for the rest of high school.

Chapter Seven
SO, WHAT AM I?

Having concluded all the studying I needed, I kept my promise to King. I didn't go back to my dorm. I went straight to Shibuya and devoted all of my energy to enjoying my high school years to the fullest.

Even though it was forbidden by school, I figured I had to get a part-time job. At the entrance to Shibuya Center-Gai Street, there was a long-standing accessory store. I quickly started working shifts there and was able to earn 300,000 yen per month (~3,000 USD). It felt like a ridiculous amount of money, but I would inevitably spend every last coin that I earned with all of my daily partying. I destroyed all memory of my careful accounting days that lead up to the legendary journey. Instead, I lavishly partied and only earned as much as I needed to enjoy myself.

Shibuya had blown my mind from my very first visit. But at the time, I only had a vague impression of what Shibuya was really like. As I spent more time there, I discovered it was even wilder than I had anticipated. There was a new thrill every day.

By the end of that year I had drank myself from club to bar, bar to club, into complete oblivion. In Chile, I had been baptized into the world of alcohol; in Shibuya, I literally drowned in it.

Along the way, I met plenty of interesting characters. A lot of people pass through Shibuya. But some hung out there all the time. There were the rich people that could actually afford to live there. There were the overly tanned *ganguro-kogyaru* girls. There were the excitable youth gangs, who believed that might made right. There were male *gyaru* equivalents, done up with make-up and accessories, crossing the streets in perfect synchronization. The club DJ, with those headphone cushions as big as hamburgers. The foreigners, who always seemed to be selling something shady or other.

Every day I would find someone to talk with, have a drink, and sometimes even fight. Soon I had hung out with so many people that if I started giving random high-fives on the street, I would probably end up high-fiving a few people I knew. All of the young people who had come from every which way ended up in Shibuya, the center of the universe. I kept a constant smile on my face as I turned around to look at the city, to see who was there. To see if they were looking at me. To see how I looked to them.

A question floated to mind.

So, what exactly am I?

To the naked eye, I was just an ordinary high school kid.

Well, no, I wasn't exactly normal! I was a one-of-a-kind lone wolf, a standout with an indestructible ego. *So look this way, everyone! It's me!*

Or, so I wanted to scream to the world. Once I even tried screaming it out loud.

But somewhere along the way, among the writhing crowd of Shibuya, I started to feel like I was the only person in the world. It seemed like there was no way for me to truly communicate who I was to anyone else in the city.

I was in the city of my dreams, Shibuya. Living the carefree life that I wanted to, basking in the glory of my youth. I should've been completely satisfied, drinking and partying endlessly, but a frustration was building up inside me, something that I couldn't let loose. I had this feeling, but no way to express it.

One day, when I was looking out from the front of the accessory store where I worked, I heard music playing. It was a song by the legendary punk band The Blue Hearts. That's when I found what I was looking for.

I don't know if it was a special occasion or something, but some place down the street had The Blue Hearts songs playing on the radio, one after another. The instrumentation, the lyrics, the singing—I stopped working altogether, paralyzed by the music.

First was the song "Scrap." The lyrics went something like this:

When you take a look at what you really have
You realize that it's not the same as what you always wanted

Clinging on to those things is such a waste
And so I finally realized I don't need them anymore
Then there was the song "In the Middle of the World":
I want to risk it all, even my life
On the very thing called life itself
The life we had before history
When humans were still animals
And the song "Crossing the Line":
I keep giving up again and again
Coming up with better and clever excuses
Running from responsibility, grinning wide
And true freedom only fades farther away
The next song delivered the finishing blow, knocking me down for good. The song was "Linda Linda":
I want to be as beautiful as a rat
For some reason, that line resonated in the core of my soul. I was like the rat of Shibuya—voiceless, no place to go. That song was able to express how I had really been feeling. Even though I was in the middle of my shift, I suddenly felt happy, even excited, overwhelmed with gratitude as the jumble of emotions in my heart made my face hot. I felt tears on my cheeks.

That was the power of music, I realized. It can move you to tears in a single moment.

From then on, I became obsessed with music. Popular hits,

old classics, songs from overseas. I started listening to anything I could get my hands on. Thanks to The Blue Hearts, who taught me how to listen to music with my heart, rather than my ears. I started to feel like every song had a message just·for me, even songs I had heard countless times before. I wondered why they didn't teach us something this important and amazing in school.

It was the means of expression I had been searching for: music, which can be heard and felt by anyone around the world through the power of radio wave. I wanted to be able to express myself like a musician. I wanted to be a musician. I wanted to be someone who laid his heart bare to the world and screamed, "Here I am!"

I started to hold back from partying, spending most of my time at my part-time job, eating simple food and maximizing my savings. Then I went to a music store, and announced to the clerk, "Give me the best instrument money can buy!" And I threw a few 10,000 yen bills in his face. No, that's an exaggeration—I simply handed over all the money I had in an envelope.

The clerk picked out a high-quality synthesizer out for me, which would become my new best friend. It became the microphone for my soul.

I figured, even that weirdo producer I hated, Tetsuya Komuro, became a star making music on synthesizers alone. So of course I could do it! I'd conquer this synthesizer with sheer might, no different from arm wrestling! Meanwhile, while fantasizing, the clerk finished his explanation of the instrument, which I had completely ignored.

He asked me if I wanted to have it delivered, to which I confidently responded: "I'll be the best synth player ever! Just you wait!"

Of course, he had no idea what I was talking about. I took the synthesizer in my arms, marched out of the store, and boarded a train back to the mountains of Chiba prefecture. I returned to school after a long absence with the intention of throwing all of my effort toward music.

The gray squares and lumps of the city gradually shifted to flat, tranquil green. I had discovered what I truly wanted: to become one of the musicians who could hold a microphone up to their own soul. With my new passion decided, I parted from the Shibuya that I had longed for so dearly and returned to the place I had so desperately wanted to escape. I felt, once again, that I was on the verge of discovering a new world.

Music can be made anywhere. Anyone can express themselves in a song. I had never thought about writing a song before, and I couldn't even read sheet music. But I still had my groundless confidence. So I had huge expectations for what I could achieve as a musician. I held on to my synthesizer tight, even after its box became torn and full of holes. It was like a new Anywhere Door for me.

I locked the door to my dorm room and vowed to not leave my room until I had written a song. Full of fresh determination, I was ready to start my new life as a musician.

First, I had to set up my synthesizer.

All right. Time to unleash my genius powers.

By the way, I had barely even played on toy pianos before. I couldn't read sheet music. I only knew one song. It was one that my sister, who played piano, had taught me long ago: the "Flea Waltz." It was the first song any kid learns after "Chopsticks."

At first, I was like an old geezer trying to use a computer for the first time. Pressing the notes one at a time, I stumbled my way through the "Flea Waltz."

I just might be a genius!

Sometimes my own talent terrified me.

I devoted myself to mastering the "Flea Waltz." Slowly, I was able to play it properly, and when I took a break I suddenly realized . . .

Wait a second, I want to make my own song!

But right now all I had in my arsenal was the "Flea Waltz." What would I have to do in order to make my own song?

I figured I'd take a break and think it over.

I played some of the songs by my self-proclaimed rival, Tetsuya Komuro. Should I try calling out to King again? I let out a big, exaggerated sigh.

As expected, King didn't show up this time. Rather, all

I could see was the face of Tetsuya Komuro, appearing and disappearing, floating up and drifting away. Over and over. No, it wasn't Tetsuya Komuro's face that was repeating, it was the song.

At some point though, the song had changed. Or was it still the same song?

No, I could tell it was definitely different.

All the different elements that exist in one song—guitar, bass, drums, keyboard, voice, harmony—I could hear them all, clear as day. I stood up, flustered, and shook my head.

The new song kept playing.

Am I in a dream?

No, I can't be.

I immersed myself once again in my own world. Eyes shut, body and heart free of sensation and emotion, the music faded away to silence. My own sighs, originally let out in the hopes of summoning King, turned into deep, focused breaths. The only difference here from my time studying was the messy desk.

That was it. I had to get back to my own world, where I had spent half a year.

I submerged myself in my own world again. Into that deep, boundless sea. Like an embryo in its mother's womb: warm, familiar, comforting. I was back, swimming to my heart's content in the world that I had forgotten in my time in Shibuya. I let the music repeat, swimming in the depths.

When different sounds ring out at the same time they come together and form something new. When they ring out one after another, they come together to make a melody. I felt like I started to understand the structure of music. And if I could understand the structure, I'd be able to make my own song.

I faced the keyboard and started making music.

Drums, bass, melody, lyrics.

I discovered their sound and their order one note at a time, and painstakingly went about creating my song. I didn't know any chords or musical notation, but the sounds started to come together in a complex way, and became a song, my song. Music was my sole master, my lone rival. I duked it out with music in one-on-one combat, again and again, acquiring my new song-writing skills.

Three months passed. I barely ate. I barely slept. But at the end of it, I had created a song.

I quickly showed it to some of my classmates, without telling them I had made it, of course. They looked impressed and asked who it was and where I heard it. By that point, I basically considered myself a professional. I was way beyond a hobbyist! I had created the best song I had ever heard in my life!

At long last, I could scream to the world: "I am here!"

I heard a triumphant level-up sound effect play in my head.

I had placed a microphone to my soul, the soul of Yohei Kitazato—and heard it shout!

So this is what a genius can do when he puts his mind to something. I'm freakishly good!

I felt like a pro surfer that had perfectly climbed to the crest of a wave of his own massive ego. From there on out, I made song after song at a ridiculous pace. And while riding that wave, I also started going to Shibuya again. I recorded my songs on tape and clutched them close to my chest as I carried them around Shibuya.

I tried picking up girls with my tapes. I would say lines like, "Hey, this is a song I wrote. Wanna listen to it together?"

I won't go into detail on exactly how successful that was, but let's just say it was further proof that I was pure genius.

But I never thought, *I want my debut CD! I want to be famous!* I was like a kid playing with his favorite toy. Now that I had managed to be one of the people who could express themselves through song, I felt like a hero. I was unbelievably happy.

I kept making songs, just for myself. I was my own biggest fan.

My second biggest set of fans, naturally, were some of the girls I met.

I spent the rest of high school making songs and hanging out in Shibuya. My equation was simple: music + Shibuya + drinking + partying + girls = genius. That was everything.

Some of you might be thinking I left something out. Well, there were university entrance exams. I did take the test.

I applied to Keio University, one of the best ten colleges in Japan, using the admissions office entrance system. The 'AO' system, based on American colleges, judges you based on your grades, specialization, and essays, without even needing to take a traditional exam. I was admitted due to my specialization.

The specialization was music. I had used my songs as my submission materials. Getting into college without even needing to take an exam felt like the sweetest possible reward.

I never had any doubts that the song creations of a genius would get me into the university of my choice.

I remembered when King had told me that if I didn't get into college, I'd be a loser for the rest of my life. I wanted to shout in his face, "Hell yeah, I was admitted without even needing to have studied!"

It was all thanks to King, who had taught me how to immerse myself in my own world. Anytime I was having trouble, going there usually solved my problems. It turned out that being able to go there was all that mattered, not the reference books or the practice exams. All of that knowledge I had accumulated and stuffed into my head, which was now filled with the Big Three sacred subjects of Shibuya, music, and girls—had gone.

I wondered if King would be angry with me.

No, I didn't think so. I think he'd smile and tell me it was exactly what he expected from me.

Chapter Eight
THE STREETS TEACH YOU BOTH PLEASURE AND PAIN

Now enrolled at Keio University, thanks to my music, I started living by myself in a small apartment with a separate kitchen at the very edge of Keio's Shonan Fujisawa Campus in Kanagawa, south of Tokyo. It was more than enough space for one person, and my first time living alone. It was a totally new sense of freedom compared to my high school dorm.

There, I began a pampered, spoiled college life.

My parents had given me a new MINI Cooper as a graduation present. They agreed to pay my whole tuition, and even sent me 150,000 yen (about $1500) a month on top of that. When I explained my situation to people who were paying their own way, they basically fainted with envy when they saw how privileged I was. I had worked harder when I was in high school.

For a while, I didn't even get a job in college. I ended up sinking my entire allowance into partying and fell behind on rent. The landlord contacted my parents, who scolded me, but ended up paying my delinquent rent.

Yep, I was as spoiled as they come.

From my parents' perspective, they just wanted me to study, even if they had to pay extra. But I gradually lost interest in my lectures and started to skip class. By sophomore year I was heading to campus so rarely that when I did go to the dining hall to get a bite to eat all my friends would gasp, "Whaaaat! A rare Yohei sighting!" It was like I was some sort of unicorn.

As for where that unicorn could be found, it was on the streets. That was where I spent the first half of college. I went to concerts, made cassette tapes and sold them at flea markets, and talked until I collapsed. I was searching for my own education and my own fun, not at school, but on the streets.

Soon after I started college, I gathered together students and adults of all different ages to start an artist group. You could make whatever artistic project you wanted, and then go sell it on the streets or in flea markets. Accessories, paintings. Poems. Our art was anything you could sell, anything you could buy. Some of the other members taught me how to make accessories, but my main focus was music. I played my synth on the side of the road and sold cassette tapes.

Pretty much every day we would do our thing in the city, and then use one of the member's apartments as a meeting spot. There we would drink and discuss important matters until the next morning. A number of them had already graduated and were working in proper companies, so they had knowledge and experience. I started debates with them: What was freedom? What was expression? Why the streets?

The first live show I did was in front of Studio Alta in Shinjuku. I set up a speaker, a synthesizer, and a microphone, and played my own songs at explosive volumes. On the streets, different people pass by every minute and every day. The same thing can never happen twice. Sometimes people would like the songs and stop and listen. Or they would just ignore me. But whenever I felt someone out there responding directly to my music, my heart skipped a beat.

In my mind, it was an epic battle between me, who wanted everyone to stop and pay attention, and all the people who just wanted to move on with their lives without the interruption. My sole weapon was music.

Every day was different. The city was a battlefield unlike any other, and I had to develop new skills on the fly. I met new people constantly. It was the exact opposite of the period in high school where I confined myself to my room. I felt like I was reaching for the core of what it meant to express myself, to communicate. I devoted myself to live shows and completely forgot about regular college life. I would later discover that those tapes I was making and selling would connect to one of the great miracles of my life, but I'll get to that later.

Aside from my time in the city, I spent the rest of my time partying. Even though my parents always sent my allowance on time, before I knew it, I would always be out of cash. I started to think that my pockets must have had holes in them. But it turned out that I only found trash in my pockets. No holes.

Just after I had turned twenty, I finally got a part-time job.

More than wanting extra money to go out, I really needed the money to make ends meet on a daily basis.

Since I wanted a chance to make as much money as I could while experiencing as many new things as possible, I picked a nightlife job. In Japan, it's called the "water trade" because young guys are hired to chat up older, wealthy women and serve them drinks. I started working at a well-established host club in Yokohama, Night Yokohama. It's known as the oldest host club in Japan. All the famous people in the city went there. It wasn't just any ordinary host club—it was as wild as the craziest spots in Shinjuku. Way too expensive for any ordinary *gyaru* to afford. For that reason, the clientele was different from typical host clubs, and the money was way better too. Female CEOs, the daughters of rich families, pro geishas, women whose husbands worked in illegal industries, and women working in the high-end sex industry. People who easily spent a thousand, or ten thousand dollars in a night. It was nightlife at its most dazzling, most glamorous. It was the late '90s, so the economy had already collapsed about five years back, but I saw with my own eyes that there were still plenty of rich people around.

At first, I had to work like any other rookie. But as always, I talked a big talk about becoming the best in the business from the very start.

Night Yokohama had strict rules. There was a clear hierarchy, a ladder system from top to bottom, and those on top strictly enforced the hierarchy. I quickly experienced the "sen-pai-kouhai" system that I had managed to evade in high school.

New employees had to stand by the red carpet at the entrance of the club and try to entice people to come to the club. And if you did, you led the customer directly to a host; the customers never requested you. So being called by name to help open a bottle of Dom Pérignon was but a distant dream. Just like how at any job you need to follow the rules to succeed, if you didn't follow the crowd at Night Yokohama, you wouldn't get anywhere at all. It was a tough lesson about society for me.

Experience was more important than anything else there. It may have been because the customers were comparatively older than they were at the average host club. At Yokohama they didn't have the flirty young guys doing the hosting—no, the younger kids were no better than errand boys. No matter how hard you worked, you couldn't just move up the ranks. Given that, I thought I just had to go to my home turf—the streets—and try to reel in women passing by.

But when I called out to women, they ignored me. There weren't women that would take a look at a club like Night Yokohama and simply say, "Oh yeah, I'll try it out." It was 30,000 yen (about $300) just to get a seat! All the kids working at the other host clubs around there called out deals for free entry. Of course the women went to those clubs instead!

But that was no excuse for losing. Wind or rain, I stood on the side of the road, advertising Night Yokohama.

One day, as I stood doing my job in the middle of the torrential downpour, a girl called out to me.

"Why don't you have an umbrella?"

She appeared to be a sex worker. Was she interested in the club? In me? Or was it just sympathy, like when you see a dirty stray dog on the street?

It turned out that she would become the first person to request me to be her host.

With my new strategy of appearing to be a helpless stray dog caught in the rain without an umbrella, I slowly began to entice people as a host. My experience getting people to stop and notice me on the street as a musician was finally starting to pay off. I knew that if your first words were impactful enough, even someone intent on passing by would stop to listen. Eventually, I got a passerby to stop by saying, "Have you seen a penguin about this big?"

Yes, it was my grand strategy: the-earnestly-searching-for-a-penguin-of-about-knee-height-strategy. And it worked. Maybe it was only because it was funny, but I was able to get people into the club, and the requests started to pile up.

The top host at Night Yokohama was a guy named Saijyo. He had gained respect for being the best host in the business, standing at over six feet tall and had sharp, handsome features. It didn't hurt that he was from Kyushu, where they have a reputation for masculine, serious men. He had a powerful aura about him. He was as manly as they come, and so charismatic that I just about fell for him too.

At Night Yokohama, most hosts were in their thirties, but Saijyo recognized that I was trying my best. So he introduced me to another guy named Hiro, an ex-motorcycle-gang member who looked after me and helped me succeed.

Saijyo and Hiro taught me everything I know about nightlife: how to drink, how to joke, how to treat women. Because they worked at such a high-class establishment, good manners were included in all of the above. They were real gentlemen, but also funny guys who knew how to let loose and screw around. So I started hanging out with them rather than going to the live shows that had previously kept me occupied—even on my days off.

Before I realized it, I was waist-deep in the water trade.

As I kept working at the host club, while still trying to sell tapes on the street, I realized that my little trick to get a few women in the club was just that—a tacky trick. But it had me shaking with excitement—my own inexperience, the many incredible people out there, and a nightlife world wilder than I could have possibly imagined. I went through a mix of self-education and instruction from real adults, and the results slowly started to show. And once I finally made a *little* progress, before I knew it, I had made tons of progress. I felt like I was turning into a demi-god.

I was back surfing, riding that big ego wave of excitement.

When the weather was bad, I skipped my shifts or stayed inside. I had an ego to protect. Hiro would back up my ego. He knew I was selfish and would say to me, "You better come to work tomorrow, then. I'll be expecting you." He was a nice guy.

No doubt about it: I was a conceited brat. But still, Hiro and Saijyo appreciated me anyway, and I'll always be thankful to them for that. To this day, I still go out for a drink with Hiro and Saijyo from time to time. I owe a lot to them. I don't feel the need to go back to Night Yokohama, but I'm thankful.

Chapter Nine
WANDERING

Eventually, I was able to earn enough to support myself as a student with my host-club job. But when you work in a business where cash is flying all over the place, you begin longing for an experience that's a little more Spartan. As flighty and as prone to inspiration as I always was, as soon as I started to earn a decent living, I quit my job at Night Yokohama. I went to travel in Southeast Asia, just because I'd never been there before.

First, I flew to India. Soon after I got to India, I found myself looking at a world map one day. That's when I had a realization that blew my mind (but ultimately proved to be unfortunate). On the map, India was only an inch wide! Not too wide at all, I thought. At the time, I figured I'd be able to cross it on an easy road trip.

Well, by the end of the trip my car was falling apart. I had insane diarrhea from drinking the water unfiltered. And I eventually realized that an inch on a world map is in fact an unimaginably vast distance. My map was a small notebook-size piece of paper. It was obviously a totally different scale from a map of Japan on the same size piece of paper. I acutely felt India's vastness, as well as my own idiocy having not grasped that fact. I eventually made it across out of sheer determination, but by the end of it, I felt an exhaustion that I never wanted to experience again in my life.

India is way too wide, I thought. *So Thailand should be just right!*

So I went over to Thailand, and just as I was deciding whether or not to try to road trip it, I ended up watching a Muay Thai boxing match. It won me over. And after some negotiations and a bribe or two, they let me participate in a match. Watching from the outside, it seemed easy enough to win, but I got beat up so bad that after the fight I could hardly recognize my own face.

A year later, I figured I would be able to win the second time, so I went back to Thailand on a revenge tour. But that ended up being even worse than the first time. I finally realized that I simply had no chance of winning against pro Muay Thai fighters.

Then I went to Macao, where I went to a casino for the first time. I lost everything—right down to the hairs on my ass. But unlike Muay Thai, where you need to be incredibly skilled to win, gambling was pure luck. *So I'll definitely win next time!*

With that painfully simple perspective, I went back to Macao. And boy, did I win big. Gambling was easy money! Fully intending to spend my money lavishly, I took my high school buddies with me and booked a charter helicopter. From the chopper, we surveyed Macao's billion-dollar skyline.

"I'll build my own billion-dollar skyline," I declared

triumphantly. Then I opened some Anywhere Doors that almost certainly weren't meant to be opened and got yelled at by the pilot for trying to throw ten thousand dollars in cash out of the helicopter.

I got back to Japan without one yen to my name. I checked again to make sure that my wallet didn't have any holes in it. To my shock it appeared that I really had managed to spend all the money I had.

No matter where I went abroad, I explored the streets. There was no time for shopping or hotels. I'd rather see the people walking by them: the open-air markets, the kids hanging out on street corners. I encountered all sorts of people, left them behind, talked with them, met them again, fell in love, got into fights. On the streets, connections between people from all places and cultures were possible. That's another essential truth they don't teach you in school.

I think what got me hooked on traveling was making friends from all over the world, trying and failing at pointless challenges, and the visceral feeling of claiming new territory as a part of my world. I wasn't prepared to throw everything away and live as a wanderer altogether, but even to this day I still travel and wander the streets a lot. Even now, I still use Shibuya (although it's totally different from how it was when I was in high school) as my home base.

Over time, the thrills and discoveries of Shibuya have diminished, but it still manages to surprise me from time to time.

I may have spent my college years messing around nonstop,

but I did manage to graduate. I only got to experience college thanks to my parents' money, so at least I got all of the credits I needed in exactly four years. I did need to get some friends to answer roll call for me in class from time to time. But the biggest reason of all that I could graduate was simply that I was a genius. As I had known since elementary school, learning the gist of things proved to be enough for me. I overdosed on my special five-fold-concentration-power technique, to be sure. And while I didn't attend classes, so to speak, I passed all the tests on my own, in person. I never failed a class. It was 10% hard work, 90% hard play for me. And I learned plenty of life lessons along the way. I enjoyed college to the fullest.

When college came to an end, I did feel a bit sad. I was about to graduate from my spoiled existence. I had lived for twenty-two years on a diet of unlimited selfishness, chasing my pointless struggles, and encountering adventure after misadventure.

But more than longing for the past, I was excited for the future. That was my life for twenty-two years—and it was awesome. I knew it was only going to get better from here on out.

I felt like I was on top of a tremendous mountain, the cold wind billowing all around me, staring down at the stormy sea known as "employment."

"See you next time, school!" I shouted.

But of course, there would be no next time.

Chapter Ten
IF COMPANIES CHANGE, SO WILL THE WORLD

In my senior year of college, all of my classmates were devoting themselves wholeheartedly to job hunting.

We were in the middle of the "employment ice age," due to Japan's price bubble collapse in 1991. As a result, a lot of students started internships and paid visits to alumni as early as junior year in order to start preparing for the tough job market. Comparatively, I began much later, but I had to go through the whole job-hunting process too. I had already decided on what I wanted to be: a salaryman at a traditional company.

You might be thinking that I'm the type to scoff at suits and ties, but that's simply not the case. Although I heard a lot of musicians and travelers scorn corporations and the people who work for them, as a musician and traveler myself, I wanted to shout back at them: "But in Japan, salarymen are cool as hell!"

I didn't have any bias against the word "salaryman" like a lot of people do because of my ridiculously awesome top-dog salaryman father. On top of that, I grew up in South America, where they hardly know anything about Japan—and even there, Sony and Toyota were elite brands. Those little letters "MADE IN JAPAN" were like glittering stars to me.

I hadn't necessarily been working toward job hunting all

through college like some of the other students. But I adapted the same point of view that I had taken when prepping for university entrance exams: if I had to do it, I may as well get into the most exclusive, sexiest college possible.

So my company had to be a company that made products sold around the world. Ideally, it would be a company that made products with "MADE IN JAPAN" engraved on them. I officially began my job hunt.

I had gotten into college, worked my part-time job, and passed my exams on the fly, without any real effort. Now it was time to write my first resume. I had many epic tales to regale, but hardly enough space. So without any real choice, I was selective about what I put on my resume. Once I had finished, I stared down at the piece of paper.

This isn't quite what I thought it'd be.

I had figured that my own resume would be a thriller of a read. But when you just glanced through it without the full context, it didn't seem to be much different from any other college senior's resume. It was lacking . . . impact.

If they would just let me explain my experience in person, I knew I could make it sound interesting. It would take about three hours, but still . . . Of course, interviews in Japan are usually fifteen minutes, max.

My resume was already at the word limit.

That's it!

There was a section on the resume where I had to write how far I would be willing to commute. I wrote:

"I'll bike from Tokyo to Osaka if I have to."

Adding that quip made me feel a little better. And even though no one ever asked me to, I gave it a try just to make sure it was possible. It took a total of four days. And at the end of it I was so pumped up that I went a little extra past Osaka to Nishinomiya, in the next prefecture over.

As for how job hunting went, well, let's just say my enthusiasm made me stand out. In the end, I managed to make them understand that I was pretty great, just as I'd done in life up until then. I didn't change my enthusiastic approach for my interviews, either. From a normal person's perspective, you'd think I was a total fool, but I got job offers in the end. Many, at that. I never did find out what the companies thought about my maximum-commuting length response.

It wouldn't be an exaggeration to say that I had paved my way in life on bullshit. And so during my interviews, I put that bullshit on magnificent display. I was like a freestyle rapper, rolling with the flow and making up cool-sounding stuff along the way without any real relation to my resume.

Of course, I lacked all the necessary knowledge for employment at any of the companies that I applied to. They were all famous companies that should've known I was a complete idiot. Still, I got offers from the best of the best. From every company I applied to! Some companies that I'd turned down called me back relentlessly to ask me to reconsider my decision. You really needed to meet me in person to understand how much of a genius I was. I was drunk on my own genius. I was too talented to be rejected from any company in Japan!

I eventually decided to work at the Hitachi Corporation. Hitachi is one of the top manufacturing companies in Japan— and plenty of their products had those precious words MADE IN JAPAN.

I became a salaryman, just like my dad. For as long as I could remember, I couldn't rival him even if I tried, but now we finally stood on even ground. Turns out the apple doesn't fall far from the tree.

But my apple tree would grow even bigger than my dad's! I'd become the most elite salaryman of all time! Although I was still completely innocent about company and work life, I had big aspirations.

Hitachi Corporation turned out to be even bigger than I was expecting. Hitachi has over 1,300 subsidiary and associated companies, and had over 360,000 employees at the time. And if you included the families of those 360,000 employees as a part of the company, that made Hitachi basically a small country. So if everyone in the company really pushed for something, incredible things were possible.

I didn't mind being a cog in the machine. I wanted to be my

own kind of unique cog, sure, but a cog, working along with many thousands of others, could make something truly special happen.

If Hitachi could change, so would society. And if society changed, so would Japan. And if Japan changed, so would Asia. And if Asia changed, so would the world.

So if I could make something happen in Hitachi . . . I might just change the entire world.

Just thinking about it gave me goosebumps.

I'd make it happen. A revolution! And with those grand ambitions in mind, I started work.

Not too long after starting, we had the traditional company training events. During training, the new employees get dispatched to electronics retail stores around Japan. There, wearing our traditional *happi* coats, we mix and mingle with the storeowners and try to sell them our products. Every week, we heard an announcement about the total number of products sold. So basically, as soon as training started, the company pitted the new employees from different departments against each other to see who could sell the most.

I had to dominate from the start. If I couldn't win this simple competition, I would have no chance of changing the world. Faced with a new kind of fighting ring, I had no intentions of losing. I resolved to win.

My department sold the Hitachi brand laptop computers.
All right, laptops. I could do that.

It turned out that there were just two problems.

One: I didn't know the first thing there was to know
about laptops. HDD, memory, CPU—I hadn't even heard of
the terminology before, nor did I understand how computers
function. All I could see looking at the laptops was a bunch
of gibberish. And now I had to go to professional electronics
sellers and explain to them why our laptops are special, answer
their questions, and get them to buy our products.

As to how I would do that? I tried doing some research in
my head on an imaginary laptop, but the only result I got was
that I'd, you know, figure it out as I went along.

The other problem was that I had to work on weekends.
Of course, it makes sense that you could find the most electronics store pros on weekends, but that meant that we all had
to work on the weekends too.

This was dire news. I had a girlfriend at the time that I was
seriously into, and the only time we were both free for dates
was the weekend. The painful choice between work and my
girlfriend stared me down.

*Easy choice. Girlfriend! No, forget that—I'd figure out how to get
both!*

Before I knew it, I found myself knocking on the door of
the office of the chief of the general affairs department.

"I must ask for a special exception," I said. "I have very important plans—so important that my life hinges on them—scheduled for Saturday and Sunday of every week. So I came to ask for the weekend off. It's not that I don't want to participate in the sales event. I do want to participate in it. In fact, I want to far more than anyone else in the company."

The general affairs chief stared at me blankly.

"Here is my plan," I proposed. "I hereby swear to sell the most laptop computers in the company. I promise. And I'll continue to sell the most. And, so long as I am the number one laptop salesman in the company, please let me have weekends off. In exchange, if I come in second place in sales even one time, I'll work every weekend from that point on without rest. What do you think?"

The general affairs chief sat for a long time in silence. I don't know if it was because I promised to be the top salesman, or if he was just confused, but he reluctantly agreed.

Now, if I didn't become the top salesman, I would never have a weekend again.

All of my weekends were on the line. I'd have to produce top sales results each and every week. Using only Monday to Friday, unlike my colleagues who were also selling weekends, I figured I could do it. Overwhelmed with my towering, ground-less confidence, rather than researching laptops, I focused on picking out good date spots.

It was my time to shine! I traveled to a mid-sized regional electronics store. Standing on the stage where I was to sell my laptops, I looked around and fell silent.

They didn't have any Hitachi laptops in the store.

Other companies' brands were lined up on display. Customers lined up, explored the different models, and chose what they wanted most. But I didn't even have a Hitachi laptop with me—only a pamphlet and my own mouth. Had the general affairs chief not known that these stores didn't even have our laptops in stock? Or was this the cruel trick of some demon? Whatever it was, it sure felt nasty. I started to tremble. There would be no forgiveness if I lost here.

I had to hype myself up. I stuffed the pamphlet, my lone weapon, into my back pocket.

I heard the triumphant videogame music in my head: *You just got a Laptop Pamphlet!* It was like the very first item you start out with at the beginning of a game, no better than a wooden sword. But I intended to use that item to the fullest. None of the laptops on display here were from my company, after all. I had to do something about it.

My strategy went as follows. First, I would approach customers trying out the laptops on display and begin singing the glorious praises of whatever laptop the customer was looking at. Then, I would take the opportunity to introduce other models and explain how wonderful they were as well. I would praise those laptops like hosts buttering up clients in the water trade. Psychologically, it doesn't feel good to have something you like criticized. It's no different from talking poorly about another host at your own table at Night Yokohama. It doesn't leave a good impression of you; it just breeds general doubt and distrust in the customer when they have something that they thought was excellent criticized. And then, with that set-up in place, I would mention just one single thing the model the customer was looking at was missing.

Then the customer would ask, "So which model has that, then?"

I would respond shyly, as if I didn't really want to admit it, "Well, there *is* a model that has that, but it's all sold out at the moment. We couldn't even spare one for the display . . ."

As soon as I would tell them that, it was game over. As if withdrawing the Master Sword from a treasure chest, I would take out the crumpled and bent Hitachi laptop pamphlet from my back pocket and show it to the customer.

"If you're interested in placing an order, I could probably find some way to get you one from our limited inventory."

This strategy hit the mark. It wasn't about disparaging your rivals' products, it was about lighting a fire in the customer— making them *really* want something. I talked till my throat was sore and sold laptop after laptop. If I hadn't worked in the water trade and learned how to woo customers, I would never have been able to keep my promise to the general affairs chief.

Thank you, Night Yokohama! Thank you, Saijyo and Hiro!

In the end, I managed to defend my right to take weekends off. My simple desire to go on dates lit a fire in me. Those laptops that I had never even seen in my life—I sold, sold, sold, and sold. Every week, I landed at the top of the sales rankings. With no thought in mind of the degree of difficulty, or of there being any sort of limit to the number of laptops I could sell, I easily blasted my way to the top and beyond. I wasn't just at the top of the new employees. I sold far and away more laptops than every employee in the entire electronics team in Japan. Eventually, they even made a company-wide announcement that I was the top electronics salesman in Hitachi Japan. (My reward was a gift card.)

I cleared the game with the wooden sword as my only weapon.

With dates as my motivation, anything was possible.

Reaching the end of training, magnificent results in hand, I felt pretty good about myself.

At this rate, I'll be able to keep being as selfish as I want, even in a giant company like Hitachi!

I gobbled up that logic. It was like an unlimited buffet of all my favorite dishes. I awarded myself a gold star for excellent performance.

I had a lot of things I wanted to do. Ideas bubbled up all around me. I wrote out a proposal for one of them and set up an appointment with my department head and presented it. My immediate boss, of course, was present. But I managed to get his boss and his boss's boss, the executive manager, to see me in person as well.

I was like a runaway train of ideas, but the executive manager was able to easily redirect my course.

"If you have no numbers to back up your proposal, it can be hardly called an idea," he said simply. He offered the criticism gently, but I sensed a strong rebuke in his words.

"Right now, this is only a thought. We can put real money behind a viable idea. But we can't invest one yen into an undeveloped thought. First, be able to explain your proposal using numbers. Then get back to us."

After that meeting, I got assigned to the financial affairs and accounting departments.

Me? In accounting? I was as prone to overoptimistic calculation as you could get. But it was the executive manager's decision. I had gone to him with a project proposal and came back with an assignment instead.

I had neither experience, knowledge of, nor interest in accounting. I understood that it was the foundational backbone of the company that kept our numbers on track. But I had never had much interest in numbers, and even when I was in the accounting department, I kept coming up with ideas that didn't have the slightest thing to do with accounting. As always, I sent them to the executive manager.

The accounting department manager got angry with me on a regular basis. The number of written apologies I sent him had to be a company record, along with the number of weeks I had ranked as the top salesman. I got so used to writing them that I wrote apology letters and new proposals to send to the executive manager at the same time. He told me to "Get it together!" pretty much every week. He even sent me an official notice to refrain from contacting other managers.

But it's not like me to just shut up and listen.

One day, we had an intra-company arm wrestling competition. I wore a mask and entered the contest. It turned out that my various life experiences had been preparing me for this moment.

I sailed to victory.

And then, standing in front of the company to receive my certificate of victory from the executive manager, I respectfully handed over my proposal in return. Thanks to my arm wrestling championship, they finally agreed to put my plan into action.

They set up a budget for the proposal. I finally got the sense that I'd be able to change our company, the first step to changing the world. I received my own planning office from the office of the president, and while I didn't have a hot secretary to get me coffee, at least I had the freedom to execute my idea. I even got permission to make appointments with the executive manager whenever I needed to, finally releasing me from the accounting manager's orders.

I ended up spending the entire initial budget on the website homepage and a poster. But since I was so eager to change Hitachi for the better, getting those initial words right was incredibly important.

"The Youth Revolution," I called it.

I designed an amazing poster with the big letters placed over a picture of a cool-looking European kid wearing sunglasses. I made it so that it was even bigger than the picture of our company president. I had it hung up all over the company, even in the hallway that led to the elevator to the company president's office—and inside the elevator too. It was my subtle, subliminal attack. Next up was an original website page. I managed to sneak in a banner link on the top of the Hitachi.jp homepage. It was so daring and cool that apparently the general affairs department got flooded with email from people thinking that our company homepage had been hacked.

I was acting like a revolutionary. But from the executive manager's perspective, I was acting like a terrorist. But no matter they said to me, with Japan's most prominent company as my playground, I quickly executed every last idea that popped into my mind. Looking back on it, I now realize that the executive manager was absolutely right—I didn't have a single, fully formed idea. All I had were just thoughts.

A bit later, I was at a company event. We had a head-to-head debate: Youth Revolutionaries vs. Upper Management.

Although my plan was experiencing all sorts of problems, I was filled with a fierce determination to change the company at all costs, and I couldn't help but run wild with it

Because, if I could change our company, I could change society. I could change Japan, Asia, and then the whole planet. I had no doubt about it. There was just one problem.

I had absolutely no clue what I wanted to change.

It was kind of a shame. I had the chance to change things, but I couldn't because I didn't know what to change. I wasn't ready.

I didn't understand the way the world worked. I just wanted to make a splash—any splash would do. So I recklessly charged ahead, even without an objective or my own vision for the world.

Three years had passed since I started working at Hitachi. I had even gotten used to the accounting department by that time and started to mentor some of the younger employees.

Originally, after my first year at Hitachi, the executive manager had told me to study accounting and learn numbers for two years, and then do what I wanted. But during my next two years in accounting, I had gotten too involved with the department and eventually stopped following my passion. So I wanted to transfer to a department that was more interesting to me.

I had a meeting with a manager in human resources, who had originally interviewed me in my application process. He

introduced me to the chief of brand strategy, and after meeting
with him, they agreed to transfer me into the brand strategy
department. I just had to get permission from the finance department manager, who was in charge of accounting personnel.

"A transfer from accounting to brand strategy is unusual,"
they told me. "It might cause problems if it gets out." So we
did it behind the scenes.

Then, at long last, the day of the personnel change an-
nouncements arrived. I got called in by the accounting manager
and was informed of my transfer. But the transfer offer wasn't
sending me to brand strategy—it had me going elsewhere in
the finance department.

It looked like it had gotten out that I had talked directly
with the HR department without consulting my manager first.
So they had worked on a transfer for me within the finance
department instead. My dealings got double-crossed.

The specific group they had me transferring into was called
the Special Accounts department. Naturally, I felt very upset
about the transfer, as I knew absolutely nothing about this
strange new group.

The Special Accounts group was made up of six people—
a select few—and was known within the company as an elite
division for people who were promised early promotions. The
members, other than me, were top-tier graduates fresh out
of the University of Tokyo, and who were already qualified

accountants. Unlike me, no one had gotten into college off of the admissions office system. When I first joined the new team, I got called into a meeting with one of Hitachi's company directors.

"I know that you were hoping to get out of accounting and join the brand strategy group," he said. "But this is a group for people on the fast-track to management positions. If you can make it in this group for a year, you'll be able to succeed at any company in the world. Don't think about it—just give it a shot."

Able to succeed at any company in the world? That was basically an invincibility power-up! I was all in.

It didn't take much for the board member to convince me that my transfer, which I had been so upset about just moments before, was all for the best.

Needless to say, Hitachi is one of the biggest companies in Japan. At the time it had over 1,300 affiliated companies, with consolidated net sales of 100 billion USD. In the Special Accounts group, our job was to draft those massive financial statements. We had to analyze business results, create essential business records, respond to comments from shareholder meetings, conduct accounting and internal audits, and more. It was a heavy load for just six people, and as a result the work was crazy hard.

But no matter how unbearable the workload felt, staying at work overnight was against the rules. They established the rule to try to prevent overwork. Every day, you absolutely had to go back home. So I often took a taxi home at 4:00 AM, climbed into bed and closed my eyes for a minute or so, and got back to work by 8:00 AM. That routine became my day-to-day. I also had to finally surrender my weekends and worked the same schedule most Saturdays and Sundays too. Work was so busy that we were lucky to have three days off in a month.

Once we got to work, we didn't speak a word. The only sounds in the office were flipping pages, clicking keyboards, and the punch of the company seal to finalize documents. I was like a machine. We all were. We worked hard morning to night. But, usually around 11:00 PM, we started to run out of gas. That became our time to chat. So, as we kept staring at our computers and typing away, we laughed and threw around a few jokes. But that kind of thing only lasted a few minutes before we were back to total focus again. We all knew that this wasn't the time to be joking and laughing around. So after letting loose just a little, we all quickly got back on track.

When you go on a Buddhist pilgrimage in Japan, when you see a certain Buddha statue in memory of dead children, you add a stone to the pile. But no matter how many stones you add to the pile yourself, demons will eventually come and steal them away. That was what our job was like: no matter how much we did, it was never enough. Most ordinary people would have a nervous breakdown. But none of us even uttered a word of complaint. We didn't think they were asking too much of us.

We understood that our work lay at the very nucleus of the mightiest company in Japan. We all had the passion and resolve to defend the honor of those words: MADE IN JAPAN. I think that those feelings were what got us through it all.

A fourth year passed since I joined Hitachi. Now I was twenty-five years old. At some point I had gotten used to tying my tie every day and wearing suits. It began to feel like they were the right garments for my age. Eventually, I was able to start taking some days off now and again, hang out with my girlfriend on the weekends, and have drinking parties with friends at night. They worked at different companies but were the same age and shared similar experiences. Of course, we all had our fair share of struggles at work, but everyone, including myself, felt satisfied with their day-to-day.

My dream job. An ample salary. Work that gave me a sense of purpose. The job was tough, but the office and work environment were comfortable. Fun parties and events. No matter where I looked, I was satisfied.

Or at least, I should have been satisfied.

On one Saturday, when I finished work early for the first time in a long while, I was talking on the phone and walking through the park. There was a group of elementary school boys running through the park with their backpacks, and one of them crashed into me. I stumbled and righted myself, but the kid toppled over flat on his back.

"Are you okay?" I said, offering my hand to the boy.

But the boy pridefully leapt back up by himself. He glanced at me as if to say, *Why were you standing in my way?* and gave a quick bow.

"Sorry!"

His whole demeanor made me smile. His backpack was hanging open at the top and all of the contents had spilled out on the ground. The boy hurried to pick everything up. I gave him a hand. I saw textbooks covered in doodles. He seemed to be in fourth grade. In a torn notebook I noticed that one of the pages was a script for his school play—none other than *The Naked King*.

I picked up the script, overwhelmed by nostalgia. I remembered my urge to be the leading role, my ego that I successfully protected. I had thought that I could become whatever I wanted to be. I wondered what my childhood self would say if he could see me now.

I felt a tap on my shoulder. The boy was staring at me. I gave him back the script.

"So what part are you playing?" I asked him.

"I'm the King."

"No kidding. That's the main character, right? Awesome!"

The boy glanced away with a shrug. "There are ten other

people also playing the King. So it's not like I'm the main character or anything."

"Oh, I see." I had heard that a lot of schools nowadays were trying to help all kids feel like they could fulfill their goals. Kids didn't like the idea of rankings anymore. Certainly, it was true that if there was no "first place" or "main character," that would eliminate a lot of hard feelings when it comes to things like a play. But I turned out to be a reckless daredevil because of those bitter emotions. They made me grow.

Japanese school backpacks are made of hard leather and close over the top with metal clasps. As I helped shut it closed, it felt strange to touch one of those backpacks for the first time in forever. The boy jerked his head down in acknowledgment of my help and rushed off. For a while, I watched his backpack bounce up and down as he ran away. As I watched, I remembered when I hit the start button on my life, pretending it was Dragon Quest. I remembered my resolution to do whatever it took to be the best. At least that's what I had thought back when I was a kid.

I wondered if rather than becoming the best, the strongest, or the true lead role, I had simply become one strong character among countless others. I stood still for a long time, now the sole person in the silent park. I wanted to talk to King. I hadn't seen him in ages. I tried letting loose a small sigh, but of course, he didn't show up.

That night, I met up with my friends for a drink at our usual spot. My friends were drinking and laughing and having a good time. But because of what happened to me earlier that day, I could hardly bring myself to talk. I kept putting my drink to my lips instead.

I stood up to go to the bathroom and staggered as I left my seat—I had gotten pretty drunk. Holding on to the wall, I made my way across the bar.

I had never paid much attention to the bar's interior before. It looked simple at first glance, but brushing against the wall as I made my way to the bathroom, I had a closer look. I noticed that the interior was made up of a whole range of materials, everything from concrete to recycled wood. I saw all sorts of odd objects, like dolls and old paintings you could buy at a flea market. I started to see the bar as somebody's secret hideout. I felt my heart skip a beat, like a child who had just realized a place that he used to think was boring was in fact full of hidden secrets.

"Awesome," I whispered to myself, thinking about how cool it would be to own a bar like this. When I took another look around, I saw a bookshelf stuffed with novels, but also autobiographies and travelogues, whatever the owner was interested in. The titles had a liberated atmosphere about them. Some of the books had been set up on display, so I could see the covers. One stood out to me and I picked it up. It was the autobiography and travels of someone I had never heard of. I skimmed through the first few pages. It seemed pretty interesting. *But not as interesting as a book about my life,* said the sore loser inside of me.

Huh? Sore loser?

All of the sudden my drunkenness disappeared along with my need to pee.

I carefully put the book back on the shelf and returned to the table with my friends. I joined them for a tequila shot and threw it back in one fell swoop. I heard the clatter of shot glasses clinking as they were placed back on the table. And then I made my announcement.

"I'm a nobody."

My friends fell silent.

"I had so many things I wanted to do, but it's like I've been ignoring them this whole time. Pretending I didn't see them."

My friends all looked around at each other and back at me. It's not that King hadn't shown up. I'd been the one who'd been ignoring him.

When I had first joined Hitachi, I didn't have any particular vision of what I wanted to become. So just as I had done in college, I figured I may as well get aboard the biggest, fanciest ship possible until I found what I was looking for. And once I found it, I'd dive into it, work hard at it, and live like a master craftsman, constantly forging my skills. Like in Dragon Quest.

If I picked soldier, I'd become the strongest soldier. If I picked mage, I'd become the wisest mage.

But now I realized that there honestly wasn't anything in particular that I wanted to be. Simply, nothing came to mind.

There wasn't anything I wanted to be, but there were countless things I wanted to do.

I had thoughts along those lines just moments ago. When I realized how cool this bar was, I wanted to have my own. When I saw that interesting book, I wanted to write my own. I had thoughts like that all the time. If I saw a movie that impressed me, I wanted to film my own. If I didn't find any clothes that I liked, I wanted to start my own brand.

It's not that I wanted to *become* anything of those things—a restaurateur or an author, a popular movie director or a fashion icon.

But I did want to craft something and have it be the best. I longed for a life like that, but it simply wasn't me. I thought that my objective was to become the person I wanted to be, and caught up in that feeling, I ended up forgetting about doing the things I wanted to do.

I had been working hard to be an elite salaryman, thoroughly pleased by any positive effect I could have on the company. But it left me grumbling about wanting my own bar when I saw a cool bar, wanting my own book when I read a good book. I had absolutely no freedom.

Even though I had so much I wanted to do, I hadn't done any of it yet, so I was a nobody. At this rate, I'd die full of regrets. I'd be a decrepit old man, glancing up at the sky in despair . . . *If only I had taken more risks . . . If only I had tried all those things I wanted to do.* Dying like that would be an absolute nightmare.

A life without challenges isn't a life worth living.

I recognized that I was a nobody. That was the first step.

There's nothing wrong with being a nobody. But I had to give it a shot. I had to try to be something more. I had to protect my ego until the day I died.

They have a saying in Chile. I don't remember whether it was Colo-Colo star player or just a drunk old man on the street who'd told me, but it goes like this: "There are three things that a man must do in his life. First, write a book about himself. Second, have children. And third, plant a tree."

No problem. So I still had three things to accomplish, even out of pride alone.

1. Publish an autobiography. 2. Marry the woman I loved the most using my published book to propose to her. 3. Start up the secret hideout bar of my dreams. As for the children, of course, they would come in due time after marriage. And as for

the tree, to me, that was a metaphor for the bar, my own place
to grow and care for.

So I let my imagination run wild. This is how it goes.

It starts with a date with my girlfriend.

I flag down a taxi.

"Where are we going?" she asks, but I respond only with a
small smile. The driver pulls to a stop in front of a stylish bar.

"Wow, this looks amazing!"

"It's my place," I say. "Come on in."

We go inside and share a drink. I give the bearded bartender a signal. He signals me back. Maybe she notices that we
exchanged glances. Maybe she doesn't. But as if to shove her
doubts away, the bartender slaps my autobiography onto the
counter and slides it over to her. She holds up my picture in
the book next to my face. She smiles and laughs, "Well, I still
think the real one is much better." I stay silent and flip to the
last page.

On the last page is my proposal.

Overwhelmed with joy, she breaks down in tears. I touch
her shoulder and whisper, "Let's get married."

Man, that sure sounds nice.

Just the thought of it sent shivers down my spine. I would
do anything to make it a reality. I'd make it all come true. I knew
I could do it. I just had to make it happen, one way or another.

Dawn came. It was the spring of my twenty-fifth year.

I was in the stairwell leading down the bar. We had been kicked out when the store closed. My friends, drunk as can be, were all piled up, sleeping in the stairwell. I vomited the tequila out of my stomach like one of those Singaporean fountain statues and stretched my arms.

Just as I felt like the passion in my heart was about to burst, the soft, golden light of a spring sunrise wrapped around me and held me tight.

Chapter Eleven
TO BE ONE OF THE PEOPLE
WHO CAN PUBLISH A BOOK

Having vowed to achieve my three new goals at the bar that night, I returned home exultant as the sun towered high in the sky. I struggled to get my shoes off, collapsed into bed, and fell asleep instantly.

The next opportunity I had, I professed my ambitions to my girlfriend, minus the proposal. Usually, whenever I went off about one of my crazy ideas to her, she would just respond, "Interesting," or "No kidding." Her position was that I should do whatever I wanted. It was a much more honest approach than praising me for any half-baked idea I came up with. And for me, it was more than enough to have the person I loved simply listen.

When I told her what I was thinking this time, she seemed to frown and knit her brows in discomfort. But I figured it was just my imagination, and we enjoyed the rest of our date.

After I got home from the date, I found a notebook sitting on my desk.

"Dear Yohei" was scribbled sloppily in magic marker on the cover.

I glanced around. I didn't see King anywhere. Was this a farewell letter from him? Since I was an adult now, did he feel like a simple letter could settle things? I did choose a pretty decisive course yesterday. I had done it—I finally resolved to embark on a path to freedom. I quickly opened the notebook. In classic King fashion, he wrote one line that spanned two open pages: "This is suspicious."

"Wait a second, King! What do you mean, 'suspicious'?"

No response came. I had no idea what he was talking about. How could making a decision possibly be suspicious? I felt like he was messing with me. And since he wasn't here, I couldn't tell it to his face. Well, I tried to ask him, but he only ignored me, making matters worse. I would rather him insult me and tell me I was a moron. I didn't like this whole roundabout approach of writing some kind of vague letter—was it that he didn't want to see me anymore?

I remembered my girlfriend's brief frown from earlier. But what I wanted to do—it couldn't be wrong, could it? Was there something wrong with my approach? I realized there was more. I turned the page in hopes that there would be an answer.

Only a fool would think that he could achieve something that he's never worked towards for even a day in his life. You're still a nobody.

I threw the notebook against the wall. I had recognized that I was a nobody, but when King said it, I got pissed off. And even worse, he still wouldn't show his face! I recognized the pointlessness of arguing with someone who wasn't even there and picked up the notebook from the floor.

I took off my jacket, loosened my tie, and undid a few of my shirt buttons. I sat down at my desk. I realized that there was more. I figured I had no choice but to see what it said.

For some reason, the next page had a math problem written on it. King could do math? Maybe he had learned back when I had been studying my ass off in my first year in high school.

Written on the next page was some sort of inductive reasoning equation:

P (n) Yohei (N days of life) = One of the people who can't publish a book even if they want to.

One of the people who can't publish a book even if they want to . . .

So there were people in this world that can publish books, and those that can't. Keeping the original equation in mind, I flipped to the next page.

P (1) Yohei today = One of the people who can't publish a book

Moreover,

P (i) Yohei up until today = One of the people who couldn't publish a book

If that equation holds true,

P (n) Yohei forever = One of the people who can't publish a book

Mathematically speaking, it was a bulletproof equation.

It was all written out in big sloppy letters and covered two open pages. I flipped the notebook to the next page. It was blank. So that was King's last message to me: inductive reasoning. I could accept that the equation was sound, but I didn't want to. I looked at the equation over and over again, hoping it would change. But the more I looked at it, the more I recognized that it was right.

Up until now, I had been alive for twenty-five years (= 9,125 days = 788 million seconds). During that long span of time, I had never published a book before. And today, in this very moment, I still wasn't one of the people who could publish a book. It was a mathematically backed fact that I would never be able to become one of the people who *could* publish a book.

Any person who has worked toward something in their life—and only those people—have the ability to accomplish the things they've worked toward. To put it another way, even if someone has a completely unrelated job, if they worked toward something, they still have a chance of accomplishing it. But people who just hide behind a shield of excuses won't be able to do anything at all.

That didn't just apply to publishing books. It went for starting up a bar too. If I had spent time working to achieve it, I could have even started my own fashion brand or made my own movie. But right now, I simply wasn't one of the people who could do any of those things.

Death would be better than a life like that. But still, I had only just decided on this new life yesterday. But I wondered if that decision was meaningful or not.

Think. Focus.

I sat up straight and arranged my notebook. One minute of silence. I could tell the length of a minute without looking at my watch. And then, taking deep breaths, I entered my own world.

First, I had to solve the equation.

Right now the equation went:

P (1) Yohei today = One of the people who can't publish a book

P (i) Yohei up until today = One of the people who can't publish a book

These are the basic, unchanging conditions that I have to deal with. I couldn't change P (i), at least, so long as I didn't have a time machine. That meant that the first equation was the one that I had to somehow turn on its head.

I had to make P (1) Yohei today = one of the people who *can* publish a book. If I could prove that, then it would, by the transitive property, make P (n) Yohei forever $\neq$ one of the people who can't publish a book.

My calculations led me to believe that I had to become able to publish a book *today,* right now. In fact, today was already nearly too late. But it was impossible. I quickly came to realize that the problem here wasn't the equation. It wasn't my emotions, or about some grand, lofty ideal. It wasn't about hard work—of course I had to worker harder. That much was obvious. And this wasn't about fluffy declarations.

It was about results. I needed results—yesterday.

I submerged deeper into my world. So deep I even bumped my nose on the seafloor. I turned onto my back. Far away, I could see sunlight faintly flickering on the surface.

I needed results.

I came back to reality. I slapped my desk, stood up straight, and announced my decision to King, who I still didn't see anywhere.

"First things first—a time limit of one year, max. I will publish my book and see it lined up in bookstores within one year. That's the result. I did it—from now on I'm one of the people who *can* publish a book. And now that I can do it, this is what I'll do to do it. I'll bring my draft straight to a publisher. They might say no, sure. Let's say I get rejected by every publisher in Japan. That won't change the result. I'm getting this published. If no publishers accept my book, I'll start my own publishing company and do it myself. Even if I go broke, I'm resolved to do it. And in the worst-case scenario, if I do have to start my own publishing company, I'll make sure that bookstores are lining up my book by the thousands. I won't be leaving it to fate, to others, or even to my own effort—it's just going to happen. And if it is going to happen, then that means that I'm already on the side of those who can publish a book! Aren't I, King?"

I could feel my words echo around my empty room.

But I didn't need his validation. I knew I wasn't wrong.
Sure, I wanted King to nod at me. Sure, I wanted him to say,
"That'll do it," but I was an adult. I could beat my own ass
if I needed to. I knew that King, wherever he was, would've
been nodding at me with a sly grin on his face. To try and calm
myself down before I got too excited, I sat down in a chair and
opened the notebook.

Impossible!

Looking at the side of the notebook, I could see a hint of
magic marker on the final pages. I quickly flipped to the last
page and saw this written in marker:

That'll do it.

If the outcome is already decided, achieving a dream is easy as can be.

*Anyone can do it. Anyone can dream. But keep this a secret between
us.*

Achieving a dream is as easy as can be.

One year from today, my book, lined up in bookstores.

And in my secret hideout too.

In order to make this all happen, I knew that I might have
to drag myself face first through a swamp. But I didn't care
about the struggle. No matter how hard things got, even if I
could barely lift my mouth out of the mud to breath, I'd have
a smile on my face. I'd continue my pointless struggle, to the
brink of death if need be.

Thank you, King. He was willing to even use dreaded
mathematics to get me to the right answer.

I finally tore off my suit, which I had been wearing for two days straight, and took a hot shower. Two days smelling rank with alcohol. Finally, I could wash myself. Finally, it was a new day. The first day where I started moving toward achieving my dream.

First, I had to start up the bar that would become a secret hideout for my friends and me. I told my close friends about my plans and got a lot of support and excitement. I would create the ultimate hangout spot for all of us. I declared to them that I would start my search immediately.

The next week I took three days off and went looking for a location. On the third day, I found a new building in a good location a minute walk from Ebisu Station, near Shibuya, and immediately contracted it out. I hastily made arrangements to do up the interior.

I got my hands on a comfy, genuine leather sofa, some flashy foreign paintings, top-quality audio equipment, and a colossal, 100+ inch screen projector. I set up a stage for live shows and a private terrace that looked out on the Ebisu skyline. I crammed that new building chock-full with everything I wanted.

One month passed since I had made my decision and I had finished my ultimate secret hideout.

On the day of the grand opening, I invited only my close friends, and we rang in the new place with drinking and cheer.

That had to be the most delicious alcohol I've ever had. Our new place wasn't just my place. It wasn't just a bar to hang out at. It was a secret hideout for all of us. What it looked like, what music we played, what kind of events we put on—we could decide it all. My dream had become reality.

There were plenty of people who couldn't believe that I had already done it.

"Huh? Already!?"

I smiled. "My homerun swing is a bit too fast to see, eh?"

I heard people shout, "There's no raining on his parade!" That was certainly true. I had resolved to smile, even as I dragged myself through the mud. I had to bring that face to the next task ahead of me: my dream of publishing a book.

So now what?

I had gathered all of my friends at our new secret hideout, and they were all having a good time. But in the midst of that, I passed my days nervous, uncertain. I had meant to come up with a hideout for good times, but I ended up using it as a place to suffer instead.

The first problem was that I didn't know the first thing about writing a book. I wasn't a great reader or writer in the first place. Still, I was aiming for an autobiography. I had the confidence that made me think, "So long as I was writing about myself, I'd figure it out along the way." The bigger problem was how to publish it. I didn't have the means to publish it myself, or any contacts or connections in the publishing industry. And on top of that, I wondered if anyone would even want to read the autobiography of an unknown twenty-five-year-old.

I had so many questions that I didn't even know where to start. But I knew that if it all fell through, I could just start my own publishing company, so I wasn't too concerned.

It was a difficult several days, but I felt refreshed after I decided on a few key points.

If it doesn't sell, I'll just buy all the copies myself!

Publishers wouldn't want to publish a book by a nameless twenty-five-year-old because it wouldn't sell. If I were a publisher, I would want books that were guaranteed to sell. So it would be easier, and probably cheaper than starting up my own publishing company altogether, to just promise to buy every last copy of the book that didn't sell. There were tons of publishers out there. So if I systematically contacted everyone, I was sure that one of them would agree to that plan.

I had settled on my course of action. It was time to get started.

I found a seminar run by heads of publishing companies on the internet and applied to participate. Held in a conference center in the luxurious Roppongi Hills, the seminar room filled up with young people. I was surprised by how many other people also wanted to publish books. And the thing that surprised me even more about the seminar was how pointless it was.

They discussed the current state of the industry. What it meant to publish. After they went on about their extensive but totally boring erudition, they suggested that we publish our writing on blogs instead. As I was already totally set in my path to publication, the seminar content went in my right ear and out my left. The person on my left side must've gotten some crystal-clear surround sound from both the actual presenters and from out of my ear.

When the seminar finally concluded, determined to not leave empty-handed, I begged the receptionist to let me in to speak with the panel participants. I raced backstage, put my hands together and pleaded: "Please publish my book!"

The first man I approached looked like a praying mantis, tall with a slim suit and big round glasses. He smiled widely.

"In that case, I strongly encourage you to apply for our self-funded publishing service," he said.

Go get devoured by a praying mantis, I thought. Well, I had known it wasn't going to be *that* easy. I'd bump into countless obstacles, no doubt about it. *Bring on the obstacles. Bring on the challenges!* Rejection didn't hurt me any more than the ground under my feet! I rushed to the next publisher. There should be someone else around. Who should I talk to next?

I realized that the reception level wouldn't be enough. I had to get directly to the top.

I had learned a thing or two from working at Hitachi. In

those complicated structures known as companies, even if
you make a compelling case to a manager, you might not get
through to the person you really need. There are monsters lying
in the deep, far more powerful than managers and even senior
directors. And those monsters are masters at criticism. If you
propose something new and risky, the high-level folks can put
out the most audacious fire. They're basically desperate to crush
the life out of you. But I had no intention of getting crushed,
especially after having to sit through such a tedious seminar.

So I intended to skip right to the last boss—and talk directly to a CEO.

For a publishing company CEO, fifteen minutes is the most
they can spare, so I needed to create the perfect situation. This
was my chance. I'd get it done.

Looking back on my life, every time I tried to achieve one
of my dreams, a monster had showed up to stop me. Sometimes
they were classmates, sometimes they were security guards, my
parents, examinations, anything and everything. But once I
defeated them, the thing I had been trying to achieve would
appear before me all of the sudden, like magic. And like in a
videogame, the more enemies I defeated, the more powerful
they became.

These monsters would be the strongest I had ever faced.
I couldn't expect to rely on King anymore, either. Those notes
that he had left me were all I needed. It was my turn to show

him results. I thought about what to do. And then for two straight weeks, I hit the bars.

Of course, it wasn't for pleasure alone.

To start, I told everyone around me that I was going to get a book published. Everyone started out being thoroughly impressed. Then they started asking a lot of questions about which publishing company, and how I had gotten through to them. To which I responded, as if I had no idea what they were talking about: "Huh? Well I haven't decided yet! Definitely hit me up if you've got an in at a publishing company." But all they did was respond, "Wow, that's great," swapping out one surprised expression for another. That repeated for two whole weeks.

But I wasn't about to give up. You never know where a connection could come from. There had to be someone with a connection to a publishing company executive somewhere. I kept meeting and talking with as many people as I could.

If I can just meet with a CEO, I can make this happen. It was the same confidence that had gotten me this far.

It's not like I intended to rip anyone off.

I'll write a good book. It'll sell big. It'll make a great profit.

I wanted my autobiography to do what anyone in business needed it to do. And since publishing was like any other business, if it did, there would be no problem. Not just no problem, they'd be thrilled! The problem was that I wasn't famous. The risk was too high to publish me. But since I intended to shoulder all of the heavy freight of that risk on my own financial ship, I just needed to get an executive on board. And just as I thought a lead would never come, I suddenly found my opening.

On one of those nights, as I kept drinking and talking with person after person, I met a guy named Hachiro Morihei at a lounge in Nishiazabu. Mori was in his fifties. In his thirties, he had started up his own apparel company and grew it to the point of over a billion yen in annual revenue. But after that, his company went bankrupt, his wife divorced him, and he fell so hard from the top of the top to the bottom of the bottom that even homeless people in Namidabashi might laugh about it. It's something that happens a lot (well, maybe not a lot, but sometimes). The drama of his misfortune was pretty incredible.

So he started lugging around a wheelbarrow, selling broken shoes that he got from an acquaintance. He went around selling shoes without soles. And with his tirelessly accumulated savings, he eventually started a Belgian waffle food cart. All of the sudden the business got on track, and a few years later he was able to open up a juice joint in Hawaii, making hundreds of millions of yen all over again. Yes, this incredible drama had a complete revenge arc, and even a happy ending.

Mori was the type of friendly guy willing to enjoy a drink even with a cheeky, younger kid like myself. And since drinking meant I gave my book publishing pitch, as always, I declared,

"By the way, I'm going to get a book published!"

Mori looked over at me in surprise. "No kidding! That's great." He didn't even ask which company.

"I'm just looking for a publisher at the moment," I said tentatively, beginning to explain my goal.

Mori nodded and took the topic seriously. He didn't talk about how tough it must be. He didn't judge me about it, either. He just honestly listened to what I said, to what I wanted to do. He was the first person I talked to who really listened.

As long and tedious as my story was, he listened all the way through.

"I happen to know someone who runs a publishing company. Want to try and reach out to him?"

For a moment I didn't believe my ears, but as soon as his words registered, I gave an earnest bow.

"Y-yes, I would love to!"

Happiness hit me so quickly and completely that I almost threw up. Thank God I had kept up the drinking. Thank God I had taken this reckless approach. It made up for all the times I had vomited from all the drinking until now.

Mori's friend who "happens to run a publishing company" just so happened to be the CEO of one of the most famous publishing companies in Japan. Even I, who didn't know anything about the publishing industry, had heard the name before. Everyone had. Apparently Mori knew him from a fancy gym they both belonged to, and they occasionally went out drinking together. He certainly wasn't one of Mori's friends from his wheelbarrow days.

"I don't know how it'll turn out, but I can give him a call and see what he says," Mori said.

"Really? Would you do that? That's—that's amazing! I just need to speak with him for five minutes. If I can just get in front of him, I know I can make something happen!"

That night, the dominos started to fall.

Two more restless weeks passed.

Finally, I got the call from Mori that I had been waiting for.

"Yohei, I managed to connect with him. It'll only be fifteen minutes, but he's made the time. Just be aware though, he did say to me, 'Mori, forgive me in advance. There are countless young people who want to publish books with us. It's probably pointless.' I don't think you should expect much."

Mori may have thought it was pointless, but he still got me a meeting. Deeply thankful, I responded. "Mr. Mori, all I needed are those fifteen minutes. Thank you so much! I'm going to give it my all!"

I hung up the phone.

I found out later that Mori spent two whole weeks trying to get in touch with him. Mori had been more generous to me than I even knew.

It was like Mori had given me the perfect pass in a soccer match. It was just like my beloved Colo-Colo matches, when it went to extra time and the score was 0–0—one player receives a sublime pass and faces down the opposing goalkeeper, one on one. If I didn't score the goal here, all the shimmer and magic would go dark.

A few days later, I stood in front of the publishing company's office, prepared for my ultimate battle. Ever since living in Chile, I had been stuck in South America time, so "on time" meant being twenty minutes late. But that day I made sure to arrive at the office early. I had five minutes until our meeting time. But even ten minutes early felt like pushing things too close in this situation. Pushing things too close got me even more excited.

Now I just need to do it. Even out of sheer stubbornness, I need to achieve my goal. I already said I would do it, after all.

I was empty-handed. Not even a proposal. All I had was the passion burning in my chest, and my iron will.

Preparations complete. I went inside. I talked to the receptionist just as the clock struck the meeting time. I gave my name. Immediately, a nearby woman stood up and gave a polite bow.

"Let me show you the way," she said, and led me down the hall. She seemed to have been waiting for me, and she introduced herself as the CEO's private secretary. With glasses and slight eroticism about her, she was the model secretary. As I watched her from behind, I aligned up my thoughts and my passion in silence, preparing for the one-on-one battle.

We entered a room next door to the CEO's office. Everything from the chairs to the desk to the carpet was top class, gorgeous brands. Now I understood the difference between a living room and a parlor. *This* was a parlor. She directed me to sit in a plush chair and asked me to wait just a moment. After she left, I glanced around the room.

Countless books were carefully arranged on the bookshelf. The books were so famous that even I had heard of most of them. It was exactly what you'd expect from a famous publishing company. The books in this room had been acquired over the course of history, won and published through countless battles. Even though I sat there alone, I couldn't help but to feel a nervous anticipation, like the books were watching me.

The door quietly opened. In came a man with a perfectly pressed suit and a sharp gaze. I sensed the aura of a relentless craftsman, who built the best and only the best, without compromise. I could feel the tension in the air stretching tight all around me. He hit me with his gaze, looked at me for a moment, and introduced himself.

"Thank you for coming today. It's nice to meet you. Since the CEO is busy at the moment, I've come to meet with you instead."

He explained that he was one of the founders of the company, a member of the board, and the president of one of the subsidiary companies. He was *so* close to being the last boss. I had to defeat him first.

Well, shall we go grab a drink? . . . is the first thing that popped into my head. The notion of commencing the negotiations over a drink had just floated in there somehow. But I quickly dispelled my imagination. There was no way I could suggest that in this overpoweringly tense atmosphere.

"Thank you so much for your valuable time today," I said. "My name is Yohei Kitazato." I bowed my head deeply. In my head, I could only see pure, blinding white light.

I had to say something. I wet my tongue. It was dry as a rock. I said something. I honestly don't remember what I said. Some sort of harmless introduction. He quickly interrupted me with a cool gaze, as if he could see right through me.

"Listen. Do you know how many books are published and sold each year in the publishing industry?"

He briefly explained how the current recession had a devastating impact on the industry. They had also discussed the topic in the seminar that I had nearly slept my way through, so I was somehow able to grasp his explanation. I felt lucky that I had attended. I needed to apologize to the person sitting next to me for all of the excess information that had leaked out of my ears.

He rushed through his explanation like a soccer player dribbling across the field. He was quick. I couldn't keep up on defense or steal the ball from him, and he left me standing there like a dummy.

"We have countless people come to us every day hoping that we will publish their books. And although we'd love to, books by unknown, fresh authors simply don't sell, even if they're good. Very rarely do we publish a book by a new author. In fiction, perhaps we'll publish the novel of a major contest winner. Or if a manuscript hasn't won any contests, we might consider a flawless draft of a novel that makes ten out of ten editors cry. We can publish a novel like that. Those are the types of books that we publish from first-time authors. Unfortunately, it's an era where even books by actors and celebrities don't sell well. So even if you were world-famous, we might not be able to publish your book. I'm sure you understand."

Now *that* was a series of powerful punches.

I had begged for fifteen minutes with him. But my self-introduction, which I couldn't even remember, had taken up three minutes. The board director had ended up using nearly half the time on his long explanation, which put us already at the eleven-minute mark. The fifteen minutes were almost up! Executives sure know how to use up time efficiently.

But this was no time to be impressed.

He had nearly reached the goal. He lined up and launched a precise shot.

"For example, if the most famous movie director in Japan were to pass away, and his son were to immortalize his last words in a book, then yes, we would publish that without question. But that's the level we're talking about."

That was a decisive blow. He hypothetically killed a healthy, lively director just to make a point! I couldn't respond to that.

But still, I didn't want this to be the end. My friends, Mori, and myself—they were all waiting for my book. Even if I was a nobody, I had to do something. Sure, this was the worst possible scenario right now. But I had to. I needed to escape the destiny allotted to me. I needed to get out from the side of people who can't publish a book. Even if it killed me, I had to save the goal, dribble all the way across the field, and score on him instead.

When I lifted my hand, the air around me felt heavy, sharp, and as cold as ice.

It happened in a flash. I closed my eyes. Emptied my thoughts. Usually I had taken a full minute to calm down and enter my own world, but this time I did it in one second.

I could see them clear as day—every letter on every spine of the books lined up on that parlor bookshelf. I visualized the breathing of the monster sitting before me. My life started to flash before my eyes. From those infinite memories and moments, I started to pick out the words I needed to say, one by one.

First, I have to show him who I am.

With only a few minutes, I had to give it my all. I had to
show him who I was, what kind of life I lived, what I was doing
today, and why I wanted to publish a book—I told him the
whole story. How publishing my book would become the start
of my new life. Without holding back any of the contradictions,
any of the embarrassments, I expressed myself with every fiber
of my heart and soul.

The second I finished talking, the same exhaustion that
soccer players felt after a long game attacked me all at once.
I felt like I had talked without taking a single breath. When I
glanced at the clock, I saw that two hours had passed.

It was a speech that mustered the might of my entire life—
and the director politely listened without interrupting.

He cleared his throat, and when he spoke, he said something I could never have expected.

"I'll tell you a story about our company back before it was
founded. The musician, Yutaka Ozaki, back when he was still
alive, we published his book. Somehow . . . right now, your eyes
remind me of his."

I didn't know what to say.

"Of course, we're running a business here, so I can't just
give you the go-ahead on your book. But I understand what you
want to do. I also understand that you're still just a novice, and

that you haven't even written a book proposal. So . . ."

So . . . I waited for his words to hit. I noticed the hint of a gentle expression on his face.

"Next week, let's meet again. In one week, I want to hear what you envision happening one year from today. We can make a decision based off of what you tell us then."

"T—t-thank you! Thank you very much!"

I used all my power to express that I was grateful from the bottom of my heart.

I bowed so deeply I basically hit my nose on the floor. And then I departed that grand battlefield of a parlor. My body wobbled, and my hands and feet were numb. Trembling the whole way, the secretary led me back downstairs to the entrance. When she saw me off, she even said, "That sounded like it went well." I nearly hugged her out of a surge of sheer love for humanity. As soon as I got a bit of distance between me and the company building, without any hesitation, I screamed.

I had no idea what kind of absurd exclamations I was shouting. But it was my first real scream, a shout from the bottom of my heart. Everyone on the street stopped and stared at me. *Yes, take a look!* I thought. I had screamed a war cry like Gabriel Coca Mendoza after he scored a goal. I felt like I was standing on a soccer field, and that everyone on the road around me were spectators cheering me on. I was damned proud of myself for what I had done.

One week later, I was back standing in the same building. Just like last time, I didn't bring a written proposal. I didn't even come up with my vision for one year later, like he had asked me to. But it's not like I had forgotten about it, or just hadn't come up with it in time.

If you ask a soccer player with a World Cup victory right before his eyes, "So what's your vision for next year?", obviously he would respond: "Huh? Why would I even think about that now?" That was how I approached it. I didn't have a telescope to look into the future. My eyes could only see the here and now.

When I heard the word "vision," I had prepared a movie in my mind that nobody else could see. I played it back to myself there, in the publishing company lobby. I was already on course to publish my autobiography.

The summer of my twenty-fifth year. The seed of resolution that I had planted one spring dawn, at last, had bloomed. Without any experience, without even a draft, I had a chance to publish a book.

During that one week, I felt like I was in a dream. A world where I was getting a book published. It just didn't feel like reality. I kept having dreams where I woke up and realized it was all a dream. Sometimes, that ended up being a dream too. It was like getting stuck in a time-loop. But it was reality, and the week passed.

A few days after my meeting with the director, I got an email saying that they agreed to publish my book. They had chosen an editor to manage my project, so I went to meet him. He didn't leave a good first impression. He was the son of a Buddhist monk, and had grown up in a temple. He had a different perspective on the world—the exact opposite of me. I had a 100% positive outlook on everything. We were guaranteed to clash. And it seemed like he had an awful first impression of me, as well. From his perspective, I was a spoiled brat who hadn't worked a day for anything in his life, someone who was getting a book published solely off of connections. Someone who made a joke of the publishing industry for those who had actually worked hard to write and sell books. The end.

Of course, my outcome was so strange and miraculous that you'd pretty much have no other choice but to assume that I had done it off of connections. For one, it sounded like this was the first book the company had agreed to publish without getting a proposal in the first place. In my case, the plan wasn't so much about the content of the book but the simple demand: "Publish my book!" Agreeing to publish and sell a book without having decided what it would actually be about was an outlier of an outlier. So if I wasn't ridiculously famous, then anyone would think that it would be totally, utterly impossible. The only logical outcome was that I had done it off of wealth and connections.

So when you think about, the monk's view of me was pretty spot on.

At that point, I really did make light of what it took to write and publish a book. I had only decided that the book would be my autobiography. And that was it. I hadn't even started to think about what exactly to write, or how to sell it.

But I wanted to publish a book. I thought it would be cool. And I figured I could do it. And if I was going to publish a book, it may as well be a killer autobiography! I had been full of ambition and selfish desires, but as for the readers—the people who would actually buy my book—I hadn't even thought about them once.

The monk, determined to oppose my ignorance, seemed to forget about any other work that he had on his plate, and took me out three times in two weeks to feed me as much information as he possibly could.

To start, he explained to me the significance and responsibility of having your message broadcasted to the thousands of random people around the world. I felt like I was getting a sermon from the High Priest of Zen Buddhism. He taught me that I needed to be aware that each person who got their hand on my book had a life of their own. There were, in fact, other people in this world besides me.

Other than me. I had lived my entire life protecting my own ego and thinking of nothing but myself.

The monk explained these things to me again and again. I slowly began to understand what it meant to publish a book, and the weight it carried. I felt like Peter Pan, discovering the ugliness of the real world for the first time. Then the monk hit me with the core question at hand.

"Yohei, what do you feel at the very center of your heart?"

"My heart? Well, I feel . . ."

"And keep it short."

He cut me off. He was like a Zen monk whacking me with that stick for meditation slackers.

"What kind of book do you want to write? Until you can tell me in one sentence, we won't publish it." And with that he walked away, his monk's robe fluttering in the breeze. Actually, he was just wearing normal clothes. But still . . .

I had to come up with the core of my book, something I could express in a single sentence. In addition to catching a reader's attention, this line would need to be something that made my book resonate with a reader, something that made the content matter. It was the single most important part.

Even though I understood what I had to do, it took me three months of soul-searching to find the answer. I argued countless times with that monk, whose father I'm sure would be shocked at some of the dirty words he could come up with. But those arguments laid the foundation for my book. I really hated that monk as a person, but as an editor, he was the best.

Before we knew it, the scheduled release date in November came and went. When we made the decision to publish, it was green everywhere you looked, but all of the sudden the barren branches were announcing winter. Finally, I decided on the single line that expressed the core of my autobiography.

"To those who are too afraid to follow their most daring dreams—lovingly, I present you with this book to fight you."

I wasn't trying to just get into fights. It was about tough love. The generation too afraid to follow their dreams had included me, after all. When coming up with the line, I had remembered that no matter how strict I felt like King was being, he had done everything out of love. Like a parent, who loves their children no matter how much they scold them, King's reprimands were full of love. Even if people thought the book was all fighting, I simply wanted to express myself as straightforwardly as possible. Even to readers who had never met me before. Just like King had always told me to.

The title I decided on was *Listen to the Voice of the Young Samurai*.

The word "samurai" originally meant a servant or attendant, but I intended it to signify how I had stuck to my goals no matter what happened. Samurai dedicated everything, even their lives, to their lord. They stuck to their service, even if it meant risking their lives. I had been able to live so recklessly up until now because I was someone who stuck to what I wanted to do. I wanted to be like a samurai.

A book for people who want to be like a samurai.

A book for people who think that they can be like a samurai.

I wanted to express that there *was* a way to live like a samurai, a way that went beyond the world of common sense and societal expectations.

Now that I had decided on the single line as well as the title, I finally started to write. My editor told me to start out by writing freely about my life, so at first I dove fully into writing whatever I wanted.

After I finished writing more or less a first draft, I sent it to my editor. At last, that monk would have a look at my masterpiece! I could already hear him saying, "Wow, even better than I was expecting. This is genius! We'll have no problem selling a million copies!"

Eventually, he finished reading the draft. He pushed the pile of paper to the side of the desk. He crossed his arms, and leaning forward with a jerk, slapped his elbows down on the desk. He opened his mouth.

"It's pretty funny," he said.

I pumped my fist.

"It's funny, and you're obsessed with yourself."

Absolutely, I nodded.

"So you think you're a genius and you love yourself—that's all well and good. The problem is that the whole draft is totally self-interested."

I looked at him in confusion. Was this another one of his sermons? He didn't sound as spiteful as usual. But it wasn't a totally callous criticism either. I could sense that this was him as an editor, honestly trying to bring out the best in my draft.

"Yohei."

"Yes?"

For the sake of it, I sat up straight.

"In my career, I've read too many manuscripts to even count. From my experience, I can say that when you write your own story in order to tell it to other people, you unconsciously think, 'Okay, how do I get people to think of me in a certain way?' or 'What can I write to make people think I'm amazing?' That's the kind of self-interest that usually comes out. Sure, in an autobiography, that's the entire point—to make people think a certain way about you. But young people in particular yearn for that kind of social approval, and it can cloud their writing. Readers aren't dumb. They can sniff out self-interest and it's a total killjoy. So you need to totally erase all feeling of wanting other people to think about you in a certain way. That way, all that's left is your serious, honest truth."

I couldn't agree more.

After the meeting, when I started to read over my draft, I realized that he was right—my writing was drowning in self-interest.

I mean, it was *all* self-interest. Self-interest equals me. I had to cross out so many lines I was basically crossing out the entire story. When I started rewriting, I realized that I was a natural-born attention-seeker. I crossed out and rewrote, but just like bamboo shoots after the rain, lines like "I'm the best," "I'm a genius!" started popping up everywhere. It was like playing whack-a-mole. And the mole was me. So every time I whacked myself, it hurt.

It's not that it was bad to think that I was awesome to myself. That was really how I felt, after all. So maybe the problem was that even if I really did have the bottomless confidence of someone who doesn't care what anyone else thinks, calling myself awesome would end up feeling like an obnoxious performance to the reader. Maybe they would think that motivation behind calling myself awesome all the time is to try to look cool.

I carefully analyzed every word I wrote, making sure that none of the sentences had any unnecessary self-interest. It was like hunting cockroaches hiding in tiny, unknown corners of my apartment. It was tedious. I spent day after day in the sole process of writing and erasing.

And gradually, the attention-seeking self-interest began to vanish from my sentences.

I ended up killing so many of those sentences that they, tired of all the slaughter, even started to leave the room of their own accord.

Then, when I finally felt like I had made real progress, I encountered yet an even mightier obstacle.

One day, I got invited to a boxing match. The cameraman who took my photo for the book invited me. He was a pro-boxing photographer and had spent his whole life following pro boxers. One of the boxers that he regularly photographed was an Oriental and Pacific Boxing Federation champion, and in that match he would be defending his championship at Korakuen Hall. It was my first boxing match.

When I got to the venue, the opening match before the main event had just started.

I looked around as I walked across an elevated platform toward my seat in the front. The music was pumped up to maximum volume. The crowd looked full of reformed hooligans, plenty of bleached hair. Right up front were the fist-pumping hometown friends of the boxers, bellowing out their support in threatening tones. The blond-haired boxer raised his fist, and the crowd went wild. The atmosphere was hyped to the max.

The opposing boxer had a serious expression, looking unimpressed. Black-haired, of course. I figured that the blond-haired one would win pretty easily.

But once the match started, the serious, black-haired boxer clearly had the overwhelming advantage. The blond-haired boxer was left battered and defeated. Even I could tell that they were on different levels. There were two standing eight counts before the referee finally stopped the fight. The black-haired boxer won by TKO. The blond-haired boxer fell to his knees and punched the stage with his fist.

"Don't stop us!" he screamed. "I was just getting started!"

Eventually, tears streaming down his face, he bowed his head deeply to the audience, and left the ring. The winner and loser both gave it their all. It was a fiery match.

I had gotten fired up too. But for some reason, I could also feel a tense pain in my chest.

These two men, both about my age, had risked their lives in a battle in the ring. Had I ever risked my life for anything? When I went to the bathroom and saw myself in the mirror, I wondered to myself: had I ever been in a situation where I was so passionate that I punched the floor, tears streaming down my face?

Men in a violent and passionate world like boxing would have the experience to write one hell of an autobiography, I thought.

And what was I doing?

I remembered when I was a little kid, I had yearned to be one of the strong heroes in manga and on TV. I had thought that I would be like them when I grew up. And how did that dream turn out? What was I doing to achieve that dream? I hadn't given up on it intentionally; it just got lost in the shuffle.

A man like me, writing an autobiography? It felt laughable. I knew that King would say so too.

After the match, we went to an izakaya for a drink, but I don't remember what I had or even if I talked to anyone. I couldn't get drunk at all.

I drank in relative quiet and returned home. The photographer and his friends figured that I got sick and had to leave. On the way back, in the train crowded with drunk salarymen, I started to think seriously about the question that I had asked myself in the bathroom at Korakuen.

In order to achieve their dreams, those boxers trained their bodies and faced off in an intense battle. The winner and loser were both heroes. An office worker like myself felt small in comparison to their struggle. I was jealous of boxers, who earned their living off strength alone. And even cooler, they sought to be the boxing *world champion*. The glorious summit of men who live by the force of their fists.

There may be a lot of high school delinquents who aspired to survive off of fighting. But none of them aspired to ascend to the top of the world out of pure strength! And there were people within the business world, in government, who obeyed the rules of society, who did more or less stand at the top of the world. I wondered what the world looked like to those who had the power of a boxing world champion? If I could read about that in someone's autobiography, I'd buy it in a second.

I realized then that world champions are on the side of "those who *can* publish a book."

How were they different from me?

Physical strength?

I had never spoken face to face with a world champion, let alone fought one. And anyone knows that a boxing world champion is the strongest of the strong.

That's it!

I figured it out.

I, someone who had never even entered the ring, someone who hadn't even fought in a ring, had figured out what I had to do.

It had to do with that dream I had of becoming the strongest hero in the world. And me, who had unintentionally let it go.

My question was: *Are world champions truly the strongest in the world?* Until I experienced it for myself, I would never be able to settle the debt on my childhood dream.

I had a new plan.

In order to settle the score with myself and put an end to the disappointment that was long simmering inside me, I resolved to clarify two key questions.

Number one: What is the difference between a world champion and me?

Number two: Is it really impossible for me to defeat a world champion?

If I could learn the answer to those two questions, I had a feeling that I would at last cross the finish line. In order to become one of the people who could publish a book once and for all, I would need to stand on the stage of men who fought and lived by their fists.

I got off the subway at the next stop and ran to a convenience store. I bought an envelope and some stationary, went and sat on the nearest park bench, and penned a fiery letter to the boxing world champion.

Dear Champion,

Please accept my challenge!

Several months later, out of the blue, I got a phone call from an unknown number.

"Hello, this is Tokuyama."

The man who I had sent my letter of challenge to.

Masamori Tokuyama. A nine-time boxing world champion. A living legend.

My cameraman friend had pulled every string and connection he could to get my letter of challenge to him.

While I was silent with shock that he had actually called, Tokuyama-san continued:

"Thanks for your letter—I always appreciate stuff like that. But I just got my next match scheduled. In order to prepare, I can't do any other matches, in case things leak out to the opponent. So I can't have a match with you. But I appreciate the letter, so I just wanted to call and say thanks. Sorry about that."

He could've just ignored me, but he went out of his way to give me a call. The world champion was a stand-up guy. I replied as politely as I could.

"Not at all—thank you so much for giving me a call to letting me know."

But then as soon as I hung up, I thought about it for about two seconds. What was I doing?! At this rate, nothing would change. I immediately called the number back.

"Ah, hello, this is Kitazato from before . . ."

"Huh? What's up?"

Having naturally assumed that our exchange was over, Tokuyama-san sounded pretty confused.

"I . . . I'm sorry. I just can't give up that easily. Just tell me what I have to do to make a match between us possible. Let's think about it for a minute, please."

It seemed absurd that an amateur would be asking a world champion to try to figure something out together. But unwilling to give up, I continued my passionate plea. Tokuyama listened to my ideas, which I strung together quickly in a single breath, and at the end, responded calmly.

"Fine with me. I can have a match with you in Osaka, one week after the world championship match."

The world champion had accepted my challenge, sent on a whim.

I waited and waited for the world championship to wrap up. Tokuyama-san cruised to victory and easily defended his title. Then one week after the match, I entered the boxing ring.

Three rounds. No standing count wins.

Then, shortly after the match had started, Tokuyama-san added one more rule.

"Fight until you get knocked out," he said. "That's how real warriors do it."

I don't remember much about the day of the fight.

What I do remember is true fear, experienced for the first time in my life. And just as fear paralyzed my whole body, I heard King's voice, urging me forward. I was able to take my first step. I faced the man who stood at the summit of the world and threw a punch with all my might.

In three rounds, he knocked me down eight times. When I came to, I was laying on the floor of the ring, having been knocked out. And I came to understand something that everyone else in the world could only guess at or imagine.

The world champion . . . is strong.

After the match, Tokuyama-san invited me for a drink. We sat and chatted for a while, and without holding anything back, he taught me a lot of valuable knowledge.

I hadn't only gotten to feel the strength of a world champion with every bone in my body—I also learned about Tokuyama-san. He had devoted his life to the win-or-lose battle known as boxing and was the hero of a quest to be the very best in the world. But even after he became champion, his hero's journey continued in a quest to remain world champion, which he was in the midst of as we spoke. Of course, even after he retired, the legend of Tokuyama would continue far into the future.

I exchanged blows with the best boxer in the world, got brutally knocked down eight times, and listened to his stories. I got to see the world through Tokuyama-san's eyes for just a moment. And from that, I finally understood what I needed to do to complete my autobiography.

Like the clouds parting for a sunny sky, all of my suffering suddenly vanished.

I was the hero of the story of my life. It wasn't the boxing match that I couldn't afford to lose. It was the battle to be the hero of my own life. I remembered *Dragon Ball*, *Slam Dunk*, and all of my other favorite manga: *Meisou-Ou Border*, *Crows*, *Rokudenashi Blues*. It would be impossible for me to rank any of the main characters from those different manga as "best." Each hero was original, each had his own unique sense of humor, and each led the way as the ultimate hero of his own story. Each of their stories was sublime entertainment. So in my own life story, I had to do the same thing. I had to reach the same level of intrigue, the same level of originality. I had to be the star of a one of a kind, manga-esque tale of real life. That had to be the story that I lived today, and that I continued to live until the day I die.

I had to live a life worthy of an autobiography.
I had to be a worthy hero.

With newfound determination, I started writing once again. A story of how my life, my existence, was truly special. Just like all of the characters and people who inspired me along the way.

I found the first-time adventure of writing a book to be incredibly fun. I loved my writing days. I loved the people. My drinking buddies, who supported me even when I put myself first. My photographer, who wasn't concerned about efficiency or charging me a hefty rate. My cover designer, who I chatted with all the way to distant islands and back. My business manager, who taught me the ABCs of the publishing business. The gorgeous spectacled secretary, who may have gotten tired of me fast, but was always kind to me in the end. And although we argued time after time, my simultaneously beloved and hated devout monk of an editor, who was always there for me. Unexpectedly so, none of my writing was halfhearted in terms of time and resources invested. All of my editors and collaborators were patient. I bet even famous authors don't get this sort of treatment! And of course, there was the source of it all—the company president who was generous enough to agree to publish my book.

I can't begin to express my gratitude to all of them. In the end, wrapped in all of their support and love, my first work,

Listen to the Voice of the Young Samurai, came out. One year after I had resolved to see my book in stores within a year, I had managed to turn my dream into reality. I had gotten the result.

First thing in the morning on the day of the book's debut, I was waiting outside a big bookstore in Shinjuku. As soon as the store opened, I rushed inside. There were barely any customers.

Where is it? Where's my book?

I saw plenty of bookstore staff standing around, but I didn't want to ask them. I wanted to find my book with my own two eyes. I quickly circled the entire store. A few minutes passed. Then I felt someone standing behind me. When I turned around, my book was right before my eyes!

I burst into hysterical laughter and tears. I was staring at my own face. Lined up along with the other books on the "Newly Published" table, my own face, my own autobiography.

Listen to the Voice of the Young Samurai

It was the title I had come up with. I knew that it was the absolutely coolest book to ever be printed. *The seven wonders of the world don't compare with the beauty of this*, I thought.

I wiped the tears out of my eyes and picked up my book. Cradling it carefully, I brought it over to the register. As if I were steps away from the peak of Mount Everest, I took each step with enormous gravity and care. My first book, found in a real bookstore, by me. This was worthy of celebration. I had to buy it. The moment I bought it, I was struck by the feeling that I had truly ascended to the top. The top of the world!

I worked so hard for this. I wanted to slap myself on the back,
rub my shoulders, give myself a big hug.

"I don't need the change," I said the cashier and wept for
joy.

"Sir, that won't do," the cashier told me, and put the change
in my hand.

I had the book wrapped to be safe, and left the bookstore,
book in hand. I quickly tore off the wrapping on my train home.
While flaunting the cover to the other passengers on the train, I
dove into reading the book, of which, of course, I already knew
every word by heart.

To the people around me, I looked like a guy who was totally obsessed with himself, reading a book with my own face
on the cover and grinning ear to ear the whole time. Yep. It was
true. I loved myself. I was perfectly happy.

Little did I know that the feeling of joy would soon fade.
Within a few weeks, I was faced with the monstrous, terrible
task of buying up every last copy of a book that I should've
loved with all my heart.

Chapter Twelve
A PROMISE IS A PROMISE

To fully explain the situation, let's jump back all the way to before I even finished writing my first draft.

I was regularly going out for drinks with the monk editor. He criticized my draft; I got drunk on the prospect of my book. I raised my finger and said, "I say we start printing an extra round of copies one month after the book is published!"

"What?" The monk glanced at me. "We don't just print extra copies for no reason. You should be grateful that we're publishing your book at all."

What an unpleasant man. But as you know, once I've made a decision, I've never failed to see it through. (Well, except maybe once or twice.)

I had said it aloud: my book would sell well enough to need more copies. Now I just had to make it a reality.

The motive behind that intention was to pay back the favor and generosity of the publishing CEO with a bestselling book. He had given me this once-in-a-lifetime opportunity. I would never admit that to the monk though.

As always, he was underestimating me.

There are tons of bookstores in the world. At the time, I read there were believed to be over 20,000 in Japan. The moment I read that, I figured it that the math was simple—if we just sold one per store, we could easily sell 20,000 books.

At least that's what I believed. But my estimates proved to be just a little overly optimistic. I was always prone to optimistic calculation, for one. As for my knowledge of how the publishing industry actually worked, I was about as useless as a priest that doesn't believe in God.

Three days had passed since the book's launch date. Over the phone, the monk gave me a sales update in his icy voice.
"We haven't seen much movement yet," he told me.

In the publishing world, that means that it was a total flop.

But why? It didn't make any sense!

I tilted my head in confusion but figured there wasn't too much to be worried about. I had a fantasy that if just one person read it and thought it was great, they'd tell all their friends and word would spread like wildfire.

The days passed in a flurry. Whenever I got a sales update from the monk, his tone and his message were the same. The numbers were *ugly*. I mean, want-to-tear-your-eyeballs-out ugly. Finally, I took hasty action.

The monk had told me this so many times that my head was about to explode. But in the publishing industry, when a book gets off to a bad start, in a worst-case scenario, bookstores will start to return the books to the publishers after two weeks. At this rate, my book, which everyone had worked so hard to make a reality, was on the verge of getting shipped out of stores.

Which meant that at this point, printing new copies was but a dream within a dream. I was like that kid in the manga *Ninja Hattori*. Not even a real ninja. I was more like the boy who cried wolf. Or Pinocchio. Yeah, I was like that lying Pinocchio. I didn't know what to do.

I had achieved my dream, hadn't I—I had published a book! But no, now wasn't the time to be proud of myself. I better save it for after my book started selling well, then I'd be able to walk past my book lined up in stores each and every day and jump for joy. What was I thinking? How stupid could I be?

Books by unknown, new authors simply don't sell.

The CEO's words had turned out right as rain. My book would end up as one for the recycling bins. And everyone in the publishing company would all say the same thing: "We should've known that a book by an unknown author wouldn't sell. That guy was just a cocky kid in over his head, and we shouldn't have gone along with his plan." Of course, what was worse was the CEO would have to take the blame. The CEO had to take responsibility. As did the monk.

I couldn't stand to be lumped in with the other failed, first-time authors. I was a *samurai!* You can tell me it's corny all you want; I still believed I was a samurai. So I had to show everyone what a samurai can do when he gets serious.

I renewed my resolve. I'd make sure my book would sell so many copies that they'd have no choice but to order another printing.

The first thing the next day, I started buying up all the copies of my book that I could find.

I needed to get the publishing company to print a new
round of copies within one month from the publication date.
That was my self-imposed deadline. I couldn't expect word of
mouth to carry me any further. Making sure that the publishing
company didn't realize what I was doing, I set out to go around
bookstores and buy up every copy of my own book. It didn't
quite go as I expected.

To start, they had printed 5,000 copies of my book, but it
wasn't in every single bookstore. Finding which bookstores had
it in stock turned out to be the hardest part. So even if I went
to the biggest bookstores and bought out all the copies (about
ten), it would take a week for the next shipment to arrive. This
wasn't an easy task. The only thing I could do was to go around
and buy each and every book one at a time.

Soon enough, my apartment was filled with books. It was a
warehouse for returns. I started to worry about getting crushed
by my own autobiography every time I opened my door. Nevertheless, I kept buying. I decided to figure out what to do with
all the books later, and for the time being I would just keep on
buying the books until they had no choice but to reprint it. So
my new life was one of constant book shopping. My money
was quickly draining away the whole while.

A few weeks passed. Just as I was considering borrowing money from a credit union, I got a call from the CEO's attractive secretary.

"Mr. Kitazato, incredible news! It-it's selling! And according to the demographic information we get from Kinokuniya, your readers are mainly young and female, basically like the fans of a J-pop boy band! This data is great news for your book moving forward, but already it's selling incredibly well!"

I chuckled to myself. Well, that was because my girlfriend had helped buy books from Kinokuniya.

"No way!" I exclaimed. "That's awesome! That's amazing!"

"Even better," she continued, "it sounds like they're now considering your book for a second printing!"

I pumped my fist.

She wasn't just an attractive secretary anymore. She needed a promotion. Now she would be a sublime, attractive, angel secretary. I was just relieved that I didn't have to buy my book anymore, which I still loved dearly, although just looking at it made me want to throw up a little. Even though it was my own precious book, I honestly didn't want to buy it anymore.

In the end, my friends and I bought over 3,000 copies of my book altogether. I could only do it because I had a lot of help from people I knew. But my book had hardly touched a single stranger. At least, I had learned that with 5,000 initial copies printed, if you sell about 3,000, then it goes to a second printing. Whether you call it luck, skill, or cheating, using my own money, my friends' money, and some borrowed money too, I had managed to make my dream a reality with brute force.

A few days later, they decided to reprint my book. And then, of all things, the CEO decided to throw a party for me in celebration of the occasion. He invited my friends too, and I drank myself dizzy. About halfway through, the CEO came over to me and put a hand on my shoulder.

"Congratulations on the reprint," he said. "It's quite the accomplishment."

It was the first time he had praised me. I was struck by a wave of happiness. But I knew it was only thanks to the brute-force operation we had pulled off.

"No, no, I just got lucky," I said, keeping my composure.

And then he responded, looking me right in the eyes, dead serious: "You can stop buying your own book now. Now it's time for us to hustle."

He turned around. Man, he looked badass as he walked away.

I found out later that the CEO realized that the sales data looked unnatural and managed to figure out that I was buying up all the books myself. Which meant that even though he knew that real people weren't buying my book, he still went ahead with the reprint. After the reprint, the publisher even bought advertisements for the book.

Now, however, I had to deal with the mountain of books that I had accumulated in my apartment. I started selling them, obviously, to my friends, acquaintances, and relatives, but also to friends of friends, my friends' parents, friends of friends of friends—to anyone and everyone I could guilt into it.

Some of my female friends did me the favor of buying it as a souvenir at their own weddings. And thankfully, they gave it away at the post-wedding party as well. Which means that some people ended up with two copies of the book. To own not just one, but two copies of a nameless author's debut must have been a true honor for them.

Slowly but surely, the pile of books started to shrink. Still, I couldn't help but feel that I'd be stuck with this mountain forever. If I really were to sell them all, friends and connections wouldn't be enough. It was time for me to get back to the streets.

I set up on the side of the road in a crowded business district. I put down a cloth blanket and laid out my books. Just like those open-air stalls back in Chile.

But whenever someone peeked over in curiosity to see what I was selling, they saw that it was all the same book, and just gave me a funny glance before walking away. I started doing everything I could to chat with anyone who stopped by. If they just stopped walking for even a second, I talked with them all

I could to get them to buy the book. I was basically doing my own street sermon.

It turned out that all my time on the streets back in college came in handy, after all. But thirty minutes of talking my heart out only sold three or four copies at most. At that pace, it would take me forever to sell that mountain of books in my apartment. Nevertheless, every day I went to the streets and sold as many copies as I could. Eventually the police took notice and asked me to leave, and after that I couldn't even sell on the street anymore.

My next opportunity came in the form of a private event at a club hosted by my friend in Shibuya. He did me the favor of letting me stop the music for a moment. I went on stage and grabbed the mic. Everyone in the club starting madly booing at me for stopping the music.

"Let's make a little bet," I told the room. "I bet that I can beat anyone in this room at an arm wrestling match. If you win, I'll take care of your tab. And if I win, you have to buy my autobiography—a book that I've sunk my entire life into writing and selling. Meet me at that booth in the back."

I went down from the stage to the booth, and plenty of jacked guys in tank tops lined up to arm wrestle with me.

I've got a chance to sell books off of arm wrestling! This is the perfect opportunity. I can't afford to lose!

My arm bursting at the seams, I managed to beat them all

out of sheer determination. Some people even lined up again for another round after they lost. I had those people buy a second copy of my book when they lost again.

I had trained myself as a kid in Chile for this day. No doubt about it. Arm wrestling was the perfect bout of strength.

Even in my breaks at work (throughout this whole time I worked my day job as usual) I kept selling, and eventually, after two years of hard work, I managed to sell every last copy. I don't know if word of mouth finally took over thanks to the help of all my friends. But after those two long years, the publishing company eventually decided to reprint my book again. My first masterpiece, *Listen to the Voice of the Young Samurai*, sold over 10,000 copies in the end.

Chapter Thirteen
GOODBYE, KING

I published a book! Now that it's published, I'll finally propose to her!
In the summer after my twenty-fifth birthday, when I had achieved my dream at last, my girlfriend took center stage. Her name was Emi.

On the day that *Listen to the Voice of the Young Samurai* had been published, and I had bought a copy of the book and returned home, standing triumphant on the peak of my victory, I proposed to her. We had been dating for seven years, and I was ready to bet the rest of my life on her.

My editor agreed to put "LOVE & SUPPORT EMIKO TAKAHASHI" on the final page. And when it came time for me to propose, I added by hand "Let's get married" beneath that line and gave the copy to Emi.

I don't actually know if she read the entire book, but she certainly never came rushing into my arms, tears falling down her cheeks, crying: "My name! It—it's in the book! And it says we're getting married!" Everything just happened naturally. We scouted locations for the wedding, and as simple as planning a weekend trip, we made our plans for a honeymoon vacation.

In this story up until now, every time Emi has come up, I have referred to her as my "girlfriend." So in case you were wondering, my "girlfriend" in all of these cases wasn't a bunch of different girls.

But back to Emi. Remember way back when I mentioned one of the great miracles in my life? Everyone might have a different opinion on what exactly a miracle is. But if I had to choose just one event in my life and call it a miracle, it would be meeting her.

It was summer vacation after my first year of college. I was at the beach in Shonan. Voices of men and women floated in the sea breeze all down the coast. My heavy backpack was full of cassette tapes of my music, and I went around the beach, selling the tapes. I had quite a fantasy about what it was going to be like: "Yo, check out these songs I wrote!"

"Oh my *God*, they're *soooo* good!" the girl would exclaim, delighted. "I would totally buy this!"

"No worries, and I come with the package!"

And then she would shriek with delight.

But in reality, selling tapes on the beach was a lonely affair.

Everyone at the beach was busy, so no one wanted to listen to my songs. I guess people just don't come to the beach with the intention of buying new music.

Lugging enormous speakers, blasting my songs at max volume, I slowly trudged across the beach. From afar, I must've looked like one of those old guys who went around collecting used cans. Or maybe I looked like one of the old guys walking around selling roasted sweet potatoes. Because I was the only vendor on the beach, tanned surfers would come up to me and ask things like, "Got any watermelon?"

"No, sorry," I would answer.

And I kept on walking alone, under the scorching midday sun.

Just as I started thinking about giving up, I had a miraculous encounter that had to be nothing short of destiny. I saw a gorgeous woman, with a beautiful face and fair skin that was just my type. I tried getting her to buy one of my tapes with my best smooth talk, but she wasn't interested. I had to put on display the full extent of my natural-born tenaciousness, and I had to keep talking to her. She told me she had come on an overnight trip to Shonan with friends. Her name was Emi.

At the time, I was living in Shonan. The next day I found her again and begged her to buy my music.

In the end, she didn't want the 500-yen tape, but we did end up dating. In all my time at the beach I sold close to zero tapes. But I found myself a miracle. I sold myself instead.

Emi was six years older than me, working as an editor at a magazine at the time. Even though she loved karaoke and was a great singer, she didn't have a lot of interest in music itself. In fact, so little interest that I eventually let her off the hook for not buying my tape. Outside of karaoke, she's the type of person that just doesn't really listen to music.

I had gotten into college off of my music, so in college I joined a music composition seminar. Of course, I had utmost confidence in my own songs. And I wanted to make Emi appreciate them. But the person who I loved most in the world, who I wanted to listen to my music more than anyone else, was absolutely not interested. I decided to craft a song with all of my heart and soul, and share it with her on her birthday.

Proud of my creation, I excitedly asked her what she thought.

"Hmm, well, I don't really get music," she said.

And that was it.

The person who I wanted to hear my music the most simply didn't like music.

I suppose I'll just give up.

It was more than enough reason for me to end my relationship with making music altogether.

Thank you, music, I thought. And from then on, I never made music again.

Even after Emi and I started dating, I couldn't stop thinking about how much I wanted her to notice me. To remember how much she loved me because of great things I did. Even part of my initial motivation for wanting to publish a book was thinking that Emi might praise me for it, since she works in the publishing industry as well. All men, well, mostly me, will do anything to win the praise of the woman they love. We're simple creatures.

After I successfully proposed, she soon got pregnant. I went to meet her parents, flung myself at their feet, and got permission to marry her. We put on a big fancy wedding, surrounded by all our friends, and we became family.

I was busy, but my work was going smoothly, with steady income. I had published my autobiography. Everything went perfect, and I felt completely overwhelmed with happiness.

I had put all of my labors into publishing my book, and as a result, had left work early or even skipped work a lot of days. But once things settled down, I returned to my life as a super-salaryman, recklessly throwing myself into office work each and every day.

Months later, I had the most important experience of my life: the birth of my child.

I heard that my wife had gone into labor, and I immediately rushed to the hospital. Emi was a hell of a lot calmer than I was. I was in an absolute panic. Squeezing her hand tight, I desperately thought about how I could encourage her, but nothing came to mind. Instead, I started heaving like I was about to give birth myself.

The nurse did her best to cheer me up, and then all of the sudden Emi was gasping. The baby was on its way.

Emi and I strained ourselves. I started to feel like my lower stomach hurt. Maybe I could've given birth to something myself, but nothing happened.

Emi managed to bear an intense pain that I can't even begin to imagine, and safely gave birth to our first child, a daughter.

"You—you did it!" I cried to Emi, shedding countless tears.

Emi managed a faint smile. There was something mysterious about that smile. I realized that her face then was the most beautiful thing I'd ever seen.

I watched our newborn daughter carefully. Reading my expression, the nurse took her and put her into my arms.

That was the moment.

A sensation unlike anything I had ever felt before rushed through me. It was like an electric shock. It didn't come from the sky or from my head, but straight up from my anus, through my spine to the crown of my head.

What . . . what was that feeling?

I felt like my whole body had gone numb. A totally new sensation. Hot, cold, pleasurable, painful, itchy, ticklish, everything—all of the different sensations a human can feel, in that moment, I felt them all. It was a sensation beyond the five senses. I didn't know what it was. Even today, it's a mystery that sticks with me after more than thirty years alive. It was a shock unlike anything else. Somehow, it felt like being set free.

I really don't know how to explain it. If I had to try, it was something like feathers entering inside me and flying all across my body. Even that doesn't really capture it. But regardless, the feeling was enough to make me go numb, enough to send me shivering, I felt a sense of true freedom rush across my entire body.

So at the same time that we had our first child, I had also felt an entirely new sensation. I was left speechless. Eventually, after happy hours spent with Emi and our newborn, we returned home.

For a moment, I was alone, for the first time in a while. My grandmother was looking after our daughter for a bit. I popped open a beer. I sunk into the sofa and thought about that day.

Just what was that feeling?

But thinking about it didn't get me anywhere, so I went to turn on the TV. But even though I hadn't turned on the power yet, the TV screen was already white.

What on earth?

From deep inside the screen, I saw a dirty-looking man approaching on a pirate ship. He wore a turban on his head, like Jack Sparrow. I nearly started shouting out of pure nostalgia as I struck up a fighting pose. I wasn't the old me. I had dabbled in Muay Thai and boxing. I wouldn't be defeated so easily this time around.

The same way he had emerged out of the fish tank way back in elementary school, King started expanding, growing, and, like that insane psychic girl from *The Ring,* came flying out of the TV screen at me. I aimed straight for his face and threw a punch.

Smack!

I felt intense pain at the back of my head. I turned around and saw him standing there.

"That's just not fair," I told him.

I don't know if it was because I had received a blow to my head, but King looked shorter than he used to. He also seemed much thinner. I remembered him as this enormous guy, but in reality we were about the same height. No—rather, I had just grown up.

My plan had been to land a good punch, and then give him a hug and cry about how much I missed him. But he had somehow teleported to the other side of me instead, whacked me first, and I couldn't help but to be angry about it. King grinned at me, without a lick of sympathy.

"Yohei. Congratulations."

The same words the nurse, and emails from all of my friends, had said: congratulations.

"T-thank you. Fortunately, everything went smoothly."

I bowed my head in thanks. And King, like he'd done so many times, smacked the back of my head hard. His blow had sent me to my knees. King squatted down to me with a big smile on his face.

"If you have sex, and everything goes well, a child will be

born. That's how it works." He paused. "You felt it, didn't you? That feeling. So, I have to tell you, congratulations. That feeling—make sure you never forget it. You're such an idiot. I was worried if you started watching some dumb TV show, you'd just forget about it. So I showed up to beat some sense into you and make sure that you never forget it."

"Beat some sense into me?" That was a scary way to put it.

"What's that—what are you talking about?"

King glanced at me, eyes wide.

"The thing that you were thinking about this whole time, obviously! That feeling that shot up your filthy asshole, straight up to your hollow log of a head! I'll teach you what it is. It's a feeling called 'freedom.'"

"Freedom?"

I did remember feeling a sense of intense freedom, but wasn't that putting it a bit too simply? King didn't have much of a knack for words.

"It's a feeling that only people who have truly become free can experience."

"What? I mean, I did feel a sense of freedom at the time. But I just had a kid! In terms of my personal life, my obligation to society . . . don't I have more responsibility than ever before?"

As if he was trying to make fun of me, King let out a loud, obnoxious sigh.

"Let me ask you this. What has freedom meant to you up until now?"

I thought about it. "Freedom is freedom, isn't it?"

"Shitty answer. Obviously. What else? Look, never mind, we're out of time. How stupid can you be!"

"H-hang on! What's the rush! If you're free, you can do whatever you want—like a musician, or a traveler!"

King chuckled. He laughed loudly. Then he sighed. "Wrong again. I guess I'll have to demote you from idiot to pathetic imbecile."

I couldn't tell if he was making fun of me or not.

"I thought you would've figured this out a long time ago. But since you're such a pathetic imbecile—an imbecile that doesn't even understand what freedom means—you just keep clucking on about it like some mindless chicken." He wagged his arms and clucked like a chicken. "That's your level of understanding right now." He clucked some more.

He was definitely making fun of me.

I clucked back at him a few times. "I, for one, intend to be free. *Cluck!* What, does freedom mean totally skipping my job and eventually getting fired? *Cluck, cluck!* Would that make me finally free?"

"I don't care whether or not you get fired, but that's not what I'm talking about," King said. Being free doesn't mean not having to work. That just means you have nothing to do.

For the same reason, travelers aren't necessarily free, either. Freedom doesn't have anything to do with your job."

"So what is it?"

King cleared his throat, and spoke:

"No matter what you do—whether you're a traveler or a musician, a sports star, a waiter, a salaryman, whether or not you're married, and no matter how many kids you have—it means taking full responsibility for everything you do. That's what true freedom is."

I paused, digesting it. "I think I get it, but I'm not quite sure what you mean."

"All right. Try remembering. Remember it like you're on your dying breath. If words don't make you get it, maybe the feeling will. Remember. Remember that feeling!"

I shut my eyes. Nowadays, I could get into my own world almost instantly. I recalled that moment. That hospital smell. The white walls, the white sheets. Emi's smile, shining like the sunrise. Our newborn baby. The warmth of life. She was as soft as jelly, and I was afraid that she'd just break if I dropped her.

I wanted to care for my daughter. I wanted to do the right thing. I would risk my life for her, I knew I would. My eyes filled up with tears as her tiny, tiny hand wrapped around my thumb.

That was the moment.

My anus, which I had taken special care to keep clean every day of my life. My brain, which was brilliant enough to amount to a Japanese cultural treasure. That feeling exploded between them and ran across my entire body.

"That's right, don't just think about it, feel it, wrap yourself around it." King looked at me straight on. "Whatever you name your daughter, that will be her name for the rest of her life; she'll eat what you feed her, learn what you teach her, and grow up believing that that's the truth about the world. What kind of person will you raise her to be? What kind of life will she have? Her life depends on your choices. It's a never-ending responsibility that you need to take on for the rest of your life."

I paused. "Isn't that the exact opposite of freedom?"

Suddenly, King launched a lightning-fast flying knee to the face, grabbed me by the neck, and flipped me over onto the sofa, where I landed face first.

"I'm serious here! Shut up and listen!"

Would a serious person really just flying knee someone to the face like that?

"Yohei," King said. "You decide for yourself whether or not to bear that never-ending responsibility. The same goes for anyone. You decide your daughter's name. You set the course for her life.

"You've taken on that never-ending responsibility for her. So you've also taken on a never-ending responsibility for *your* own life. Freedom is not what you think it is. True freedom only comes with true responsibility. Up until now, whether it was your parents back in school, or your boss at work, you've been someone else's responsibility. You may not have realized it, but somewhere along the way, you've compared your own perspective with the way the world and society thinks. You've searched for a way to live, a way to be, and adjusted your life along the way to fit.

"And the way that you've decided to go through life is to disregard common sense and responsibility. You've always considered what 'common sense' is and then thrown it out because you believed in doing what you want to do—but you can't forget about responsibility. Even though you've accomplished a lot, you still don't quite understand. That's why I'm here now. Do you get it yet?"

King sat brazenly on top of our coffee table with his legs open, like some kind of bold samurai, staring at me. I righted myself on the sofa and faced King.

"I think I get it." I nodded. Now I understood why I hadn't seen King in so long. Everything was going well, and I was happy in life, but one small bit at a time, I had started to slide into society, just like everyone else. I felt like I needed to apologize to him.

King must have looked the way he did—dirty as a sailor and thinner than ever—because I hadn't been following what he taught me. Being the way he is, maybe he went out looking for something, on some journey or other, and stopped caring about me. I started to raise my voice but that one, simple word, *Sorry*, just wouldn't leave my throat. Somewhere along the line I had lost the unfiltered honesty that I had in childhood.

I don't know if it was because he realized what I was going through, but all of the sudden he smiled. It was a smile I had never seen from him before. His face lit up with an expression of pure love, and, at the same time, an expression of pure sorrow.

"Listen, Yohei," King said. "In this messed up world, you've done a damned good job at protecting your ego. I admire you for that. You may be pathetically stupid, but you're not a complete waste of space. You've found true freedom. You did it. Run with it. Believe that you're invincible the rest of your life. From now on, you're the captain of your own ship."

I didn't know what to say.

"I think you already understand what's happening, but this is the last time I'll see you. So I'll give you one last piece of advice."

I nodded.

"True freedom brings with it uncertainty. Because you can't control everything. But you can do anything, and you're allowed to fail."

"When you're somebody else's responsibility and you have stability, you can control everything around you, so there's no way that you can fail. In a way, you can't do anything at all. You're not free. This world is full of paradoxes. You work at a company, get health insurance, save up money, and you feel stable and safe, but still you think, 'man, wouldn't it be nice to be free?' Go, try being stable now—you'll realize just how unfree you are.

"But now you're the captain of your own ship. You set the course of your own life on this new ship called freedom. Sure, there's tons of uncertainty. You might sink your ship. But so what? Then swim. Get a new ship. That much, I'm sure you can do. Enjoy the uncertainty. Sail the seas."

I felt his words echo inside of me. I carved them into my heart.

But I couldn't get over the fact that this was the last time I'd ever see him.

"All right, I'm off."

"Where?" I asked.

"I won't ever see you again. From this moment on, you're me, and I'm you. You've been searching for this ship all your life, haven't you? Well now you've boarded it. You don't need anyone else's ship—you have your own. Your family is your ship. Something you'll have for the rest of your life, something that never leaves you. Something worth dying for, if need be. You're the captain of that ship.

"You may not be the Naked King, but you've gotten a different leading role as captain. And now you're going to sail the stormy seas of life. You'll shoulder never-ending responsibility, spurred on by sails of love. Holding dearly to the helm of freedom, you'll decide the course."

He bowed his head. "I enjoyed our life together."

Then in an instant, King vanished from my sight. There was no smoke, no smell, no trace of him at all. Flustered, I had run toward him to try and hold onto him, but there had been nothing to grab. The TV was off, the room was silent. I stood there, alone.

I cleared my throat and tried to speak. The words got caught in my throat.

Even though he knew full well what I wanted and needed to tell him, he disappeared anyway, for good. Before I could tell him.

All the time I had spent with him, ever since elementary school. All the pain from his punches. All of the times I thought so hard that smoke started coming out of my ears. All of the times he clapped my shoulders with joy. Even though I could remember each and every one of those times as vividly as if it had happened yesterday, I knew that I would never experience them again.

And although he was the one who had gotten me through so much, I'd never given him a proper thanks, not even once. And despite all of the times I'd ignored his advice and driven him to exhaustion and disappointment, I'd never given him a proper apology, either.

"Look . . . I'm sorry. But . . . thank you."

I started to mutter the words aloud, like a small child who barely knew how to speak. I'm sorry, thank you, I'm sorry, thank you, over and over. My voice was hoarse, trembling. I kept trying to tell him, to express how I felt, but quickly my words crumbled into sobs and tears started to fall out of my eyes. My tears were still searching for him. So without even wiping them away, I sat there and wailed like an injured child.

King had taught me so many things, but he had never told me how to stop myself from crying.

From that day on, King never appeared again.

A few weeks later, I handed in my letter of resignation.

It wasn't that my job hadn't been fulfilling. They had let me get in way over my head with important work, and I always felt like the work had a sense of purpose. I had learned priceless lessons only because I had belonged to one of those massive organizations known as a corporation. Before my job, I had gone about my life without thinking twice about it like a monkey, and working for Hitachi had turned me into a real homo sapien. I'm still sure someday Hitachi will make a real impact on society.

To return to that metaphor of the ship, you could say that up until now, I had been a sailor aboard the Hitachi vessel, as massive and splendid as the *Titanic*. Of course, I liked the ship. All the sailors kept working their hardest, and the voyage went on. But I had a family to protect. If I brought my family aboard the *Titanic* with me, and in the worst-case scenario that the massive ship sunk, we'd all go down with it. I had no intention of being one of the heroic sailors who stayed on the ship to the bitter end. I intended to get a rescue boat and escape with my family before the ship sunk.

Since I wasn't prepared to commit to the ship that I was on, I wouldn't be able to continue this voyage in good faith. I went around making my sincere apologies and offering gratitude to all of my coworkers, and at last, left Hitachi behind.

But let me backtrack a bit.

With my letter of resignation in hand, I went to the office of one of the company board directors. I knocked carefully, and then opened the door.

"Pardon the interruption," I said. "Can I talk to you for a moment?"

"What is it?"

The board director, who had been my supervisor and had helped me out time and time again, looked up from his desk.

"We just had a baby," I told him. "Starting today, I've decided to take life more seriously."

My boss raised his eyebrows. He looked at me for a moment. "So you've become an adult now, I see? That's good. Now you can work even harder."

"Along those lines, I've also made the decision to leave the company."

My boss had "Is this guy insane?" written all over his face.

I went on to explain the full story of why I wanted to quit.

"So what are you going to do for a living?" he asked.

I puffed up my chest.

"I'm going to create my own publishing company!"

Yup. I planned to start up my own publishing business soon after I quit.

I wanted to make sure that the responsibility for my own family lay squarely on my own shoulders. It was time to get my own ship. And of course, I'd be the captain.

I had resolved firmly to do what I thought was necessary from here on out. I'd sail free in this world to my heart's content, wherever the wind might lead my ship.

The ship's name would be NORTH VILLAGE. (It was the English translation of my last name, Kitazato.)

I started off by borrowing sixteen million yen (about 160 thousand dollars) to start up my publishing company. Then, after the fact, I revealed it all to my beloved wife.

"I've quit my job," I declared to her.

Holding our baby in her arms, she simply bobbed her head. "Okay."

That was all she said. Her reaction wouldn't have been any different if I told her it was snowing outside. But since nothing tended to surprise Emi at this point, it was a reasonable reaction for her.

"So I've been thinking about starting up a publishing company, but since I don't have enough savings on hand, I borrowed sixteen million yen," I continued.

"Wow," she said.

I looked at her. "Uh . . . is that your reaction?"

At the moment, she appeared more focused on cuddling the baby. I had never taken out a big loan like that before and had been grappling to understand the gravity of the situation myself. A huge loan like that—I assumed that even Emi would be furious at me for not telling her beforehand.

Emi looked up at me. "Well, you've already decided to do it, haven't you?"

I nodded. And that was the end of the discussion.

Two weeks later, Emi suddenly asked me, "So, how much do you have to pay back on the loan each month?"

"Huh? Why?" I hadn't expected her to bring it up.

"If something happens to you, I'd be the one who'd have to pay it back. We're family now. So I figured that I better know how much exactly we need to be paying."

"It's an unsecured, unguaranteed loan. So even if I die, you don't have to pay it back," I told her. I didn't want her to have to worry about it.

But she responded, "That doesn't make sense. It's not right. I want to pay it back, so just tell me how much."

I could never lie to her. So I told her straight up the monthly amount.

It was no small sum. I suddenly felt my heart racing, unsure what her reaction might be, but she replied calmly.

"Okay, got it." End of conversation. Once again, everything ended with a simple "okay."

After that, she never asked me about the company finances or anything about work at all. I fell head over heels for that woman. The partner I had chosen was perfect for me, on the outside and inside. I knew she was the perfect wife.

Epilogue
NORTH VILLAGE

Ten years have passed since I started my new voyage. Since then, I've had two more kids, making me an unlikely father of three.

It was my new voyage, across the stormy seas of the publishing world. I went on making decisions for myself, taking full responsibility for my decisions, setting my own course. At first, I had the enthusiasm, but lacked pretty much everything else—experience, skill, connections, and funds. All of that contributed to how making North Village a reality ended up being a far greater challenge than I had anticipated.

So let me tell you a little bit about North Village and what we're up to.

I'm pretty sure it's not an actual profession, but I had decided to be a professional autobiographer. I set out on a path of gathering up all of my stories, all of my actions, all of my feelings, and putting them into a book with me as the star.

I had started up a publishing company because I figured that if I was going to make my life's work writing whatever book I wanted, whenever I wanted, without anyone to complain about it to me, starting up my own publishing company would be the soundest solution. But soon after, I started to set my sights even higher. I wanted to travel around the world and write about my experiences and make those journeys and my stories about them my life's work. And once I got back from those travels, I'd gather my buddies at my secret base and tell them all about it. Plenty of people laughed in my face and told me it was impossible, but I never doubted that I couldn't achieve it, even for a second. I had given up on giving up, after all.

One day, when North Village had finally gotten on the right track, I knew that all of my dreams would come true. I began the adventure with the purest conviction that I was invincible.

If I tried to achieve it all, I was convinced that the company would start pulling in money sooner or later. Of course, I knew that I would run into countless obstacles for years. I burned through the start-up loan of sixteen million yen within a few months. It would take seven full months before I got North Village's first book published and saw any revenue at all. If the book didn't sell, then I wouldn't make anything despite the seven months of work. And then, even if it did, I had to pay off all of my expenses first before I got to keep any of that money for myself. I didn't realize any of these complications until about six months of working on the company. Before I knew it, I had taken out 50 million yen in loans.

But it's wasn't right that my family had to live poorly just because I was doing what I wanted to do. Freedom meant protecting my family at all cost. So I pretended to Emi that we always had money. We didn't lower the standard of living from when I was a salaryman. We continued to live in relative luxury, wanting for nothing.

Still, with all the loans, my monthly payments ended up being about four million yen (40,000 dollars). The company had no income. So since I couldn't even come close to making the payments, we figured it wouldn't hurt if our family expenses were on the high side, either. The situation didn't change for nearly two and a half years.

Two and a half years later, North Village, which had started from nothing, now earned a couple hundred thousand yen per month (a few thousand dollars). In terms of Dragon Quest, it felt like going from one of the tough bosses (Baramos) to the final boss (Zoma), month after month after month. Paying each month's expenses was a struggle to the death, and I couldn't even look ahead to the next month.

But eventually the day came when I flipped the switch for good.

On that day, a month passed where I had no money left after paying all the business expenses, and I wasn't able to make our loan payments. As I walked over a pedestrian bridge toward Shibuya Station, a thought popped into mind.

How the hell does a company even earn money in the first place? Estimating quotes, establishing contracts, submitting invoices . . . What a pain.

I stopped in the middle of the bridge and looked down at the swarming people and business suits below.

I always figured they were all salaryman working for some company, but a lot of them might be freelancers or entrepreneurs. They're all working hard to make it on just 200 or 300 thousand yen a month . . . that's pretty amazing.

For the sake of it, I imagined that all of those commuters weren't salarymen, but freelancers. Every day they were estimating quotes, making contracts, mailing invoices—rinse and repeat—earning enough to support their families, pay their rent, live their lives. From that perspective, even the ordinary scene of Shibuya Station started to look like a primitive, wild jungle.

They're amazing!

They were wild animals, hunting for prey to feed themselves and their families. Right here at Shibuya Station.

The world is more primitive than I thought. I can't let myself be someone else's prey.

It was a shocking realization. And that's when I managed to flip the switch.

From then on, in addition to the publishing company's main business of trying to connect with famous people to publish their books, I started doing anything and everything else to get by. I had a few million yen per month in payments, after all, so I began my ruthless war to pay those dues in full every time.

To start off, I went to bars. I chatted up all sorts of people, got introductions to any CEO or business owner that they knew. I introduced myself, and said these magic words: "If I could do anything for you—anything in the world, possible or not—what would you have me do?"

These CEOs, from a variety of backgrounds and industries, almost always told me about something that their teams hadn't been able to do and had given up on. I gave them a simple proposal: If I take your wish and make it happen in two weeks or less, will you pay me four million yen the following day?

Four million yen is a very expensive service. I was trying to make in two weeks what a salaryman typically makes in a year. Given the difficulty of the tasks, this was pretty much an unbeatable game. And with a two-week limit, on top it all. Sometimes, worse than unbeatable, the tasks were as outrageous as a punch to the face. But in this game I had invented for myself, my controller only had a start button. No matter how sticky a situation you're in, you can usually get out of it if you just press start. My life is solid proof of that.

I'm not going to get into all of the details, but here are a few of the tasks.

Client: hat shop owner. Mission: Sell out the remaining inventory of 40,000 hats.

Client: small advertising agency. Mission: Win a contract to make a TV commercial for a large corporation.

Client: a regional accounting firm. Mission: Find a three-million-yen local contract.

Client: publishing company. Mission: Sell two years' worth of ads for a magazine.

Client: volunteer organization. Mission: Set up collection boxes in 1,000 locations.

How exactly I managed to clear each of those missions would require novels of their own.

Sooner or later North Village will put out a bestseller! I thought, and resolved to keep on clearing missions for CEOs until my company could get by on its book sales. That was my life for two and a half years.

It was a tempestuous period. Then, I published *Dreams Don't Run Away. Only You Do* by Ayumu Takahashi in 2010. It became a bestseller, and finally I could wash my hands of the whole mission-clearing business.

At North Village I never published my own autobiography. I went around to artists and businesspeople and people who I admired in all different fields. I charmed them as best I could and started to turn their stories into books and sell them.

So why did I put off my own autobiography in favor of theirs?

I knew that a day would come when North Village would publish my autobiography, and I'd see it lined up in bookstores all around Japan. I had already decided that I would make it happen. But when that day came, I didn't want to see my book lined up on those shelves alone. So I convinced people with my own wit to join me in making great, bestselling books. I wanted to see it lined up alongside people who I respected and admired. Now *that* would be the absolute bomb.

The books of writers I admired slowly filled my bookshelf. While I worked with them to create books, I also learned so much from them, not unlike my time with King. There was Shigeo Hamada, Ayumu Takahashi, the writer and radio producer Robert Harris, the actor Masayuki Yui, Kazuma Ieiri, the founder of "paperboy," the actor Yosuke Kubozuka, even the star musician GACKT. They were all my life teachers. And North Village gave life to their work.

Yosuke Kubozuka and I were about the same age, so we started a series of books where we traveled together and wrote about it, which continued for several years. Yosuke was so cool. He had just made his Hollywood debut, sidelined as a reggae DJ, had an incredibly cool aesthetic, believed in himself, and never stopped taking on new challenges. Beyond our time traveling together, he's had a big influence on my life as a whole.

After I stopped doing my CEO missions, I started up new lines of business for North Village. As always, I wanted a new challenge. Most important of all, if I could make money off of doing something, I may as well go for it and enjoy the fun of it along the way.

For example, I opened a unique thrift store.

One day, a friend invited me to an antique auction. In the

midst of the impassioned bidding, I truly came to understand how one man's trash can be another man's treasure. I realized that it's much more exciting to shop in an auction setting and got a permit to sell antiques myself.

My friend Jiro Matsui, who lived in Nagoya at the time, moved to Tokyo and helped me launch a "24 Hour Auction" thrift store. For the first time, North Village had a full-time employee other than myself. Twenty-four hours a day, 365 days a year, selling everything and anything imaginable, we made the shop into a success out of sheer willpower. Now we have over one million listed items annually.

Then there was the shisha cafe.

Yosuke and I went to Egypt on one of our trips to write a book. Our second morning there, we went to the cafe in our hotel. Yosuke tried shisha tobacco, which had its origins in Egyptian culture. I didn't smoke, but because Yosuke recommended it, I gave it a try.

Immediately we bought shisha and brought it back to my secret hideout. We rented out some hookah gear to set things up and launched a shisha cafe the day after we got back to Japan. Our concept was a place to drink, enjoy yourself, and smoke some hookah. So we rigged it up with some comfy, used chairs and sofas from the thrift store. Right in front of the chairs, we made sure to set up a large bookshelf with the books North Village had published so far. I had officially taken my secret hideout, which I had been fantasizing about and loving since my mid-twenties, to the next level.

As I kept gathering friends for our book launches in my secret hideout, everyone checked out and loved the shisha cafe. It was so successful that we expanded to seventeen shisha locations in Tokyo over the next five years alone. We made partnerships with some foreign companies to make custom tobacco flavors, and soon enough, we got a lot of business coming through the shisha cafe.

Right now I'm working on a new initiative to go global. We're hoping to launch shisha cafe booths in Machu Picchu and Malaysia. I have a feeling that once we get those launched, all sorts of adventures will begin all over again.

There was also the real estate agency.

As I worked on expanding the shisha cafe, I grew to understand the pure fun of looking for a property more and more. So I started up a real estate agency called "Tokyo Secret Base." This is a brand-new enterprise, but our mission is to help people find a place that they think is the ultimate hideout for their shop, office, or residence. It would also enable us to start launching locations for the shisha cafes all around Japan.

In the ten years that have passed since launching North Village, including part-time workers, we've employed over eighty people. We sail the seas of publishing, recycling, shisha, and real estate, and our adventures are far from over.

Well then, this long story has come to an end.

What exactly *is* my job, you ask?

I can tell you there's no business card for it. I'm an autobiographer. It may not be a real profession. But that's what I am.

In terms of Dragon Quest, I suppose that makes me a jester, or a Gadabout.

I spend half of my time in Japan, split between my family and hanging out at my secret base. The other half of the time, I travel the world, writing books.

That's me, a professional Gadabout.

I turn my work into my play, and work and play with everything I have. My family and my company have grown, and while it's not easy, every day is fulfilling. I've gotten to where I am off of trial and error, for sure, but there's one important theme that stands out.

I *want to make Emi fall in love with me all over again.*

That has been the biggest mission in my life.

While my kids are at school, sometimes Emi and I go to the supermarket together. Even now, twenty years after meeting her, I still can't keep my composure when I'm around her. I'll try to hold her hand, and she'll pull her hand away, saying, "Not in the neighborhood, it's embarrassing if the other moms see," and it leaves me absolutely devastated.

Whenever we're together, I feel the same way I did on our very first date. While she's looking at groceries, carefully deciding what to buy in the interest of our family, one look at her profile makes my heart skip a beat. It's the same way I felt the day I met her at Shonan Beach.

Emi—the woman sees right through me. More than any other challenge I've ever faced, making her stay in love with me has been the most difficult of them all.

I constantly want to show her a new side of me that I've never displayed before and have her fall in love with me all over again. But now, twenty years later, there's no more of me left to show.

All I can do is keep growing, doing new things, and making new, cooler sides of myself to impress her.

And you kids!

I'm working hard every day to make sure your mother loves me even in the next life. It's more important than studying or work.

I've digressed. It's a bad habit of mine to keep rambling on.

But on the other hand, there are still so many more adventures to talk about. North Village's next launch. My next autobiography.

I know I'm going to keep writing autobiographies for the rest of my life. I'm going to keep living a life worthy of them.

In Dragon Quest, when a Gadabout, reaches level 20, it can be promoted into a sage. But not me. I'm going to keep messing around and having fun my whole life, even when I'm level 99. *That* is my pointless struggle.

As promised, King never did show up again.

Am I lonely?

No, not at all. Because when I look in the mirror, I can see him smiling back at me.

Yohei Kitazato's Journey Continues

One more thing.

This book is another dream come true. In fact, it's two dreams come true: my dream of growing up to be a hero in a manga that I had as a little kid, and the dream I had as an adult of being the hero of my own autobiography.

I extend my utmost gratitude to the manga artist Akio Tanaka for making this a reality. Thank you from the bottom of my heart!

And, as always, to Emi and the kids, who are always there for me, to Mom and Dad, to Erika, Grandmother, Toto, the North Village crew who makes everything happen, to the authors who publish books through us, and last but not least, and last but not least, to all of my readers and all of my friends:

Thank you!

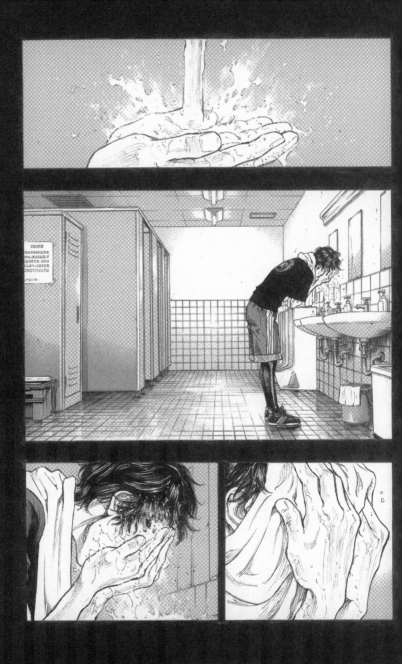

ABOUT THE AUTHOR

Yohei Kitazato was born in Japan and raised in Chile. After graduating from the Keio University, he joined Hitachi, one of Japan's largest companies. While employed at Hitachi, Kitazato opened his own bar, and published his first book, *Listen to the Voice of the Young Samurai*. Shortly after, he launched his own start-up publishing company, North Village. There Kitazato sought out authors he respected and published their autobiographies. The company has since released multiple best-selling titles. Currently, in addition to North Village, Kitazato is operating twenty hookah lounges around the world in locations as far flung as Macchu Picchu and Kuala Lumpur. With a working style that turns his passions into a career, he also runs a 24-7 consignment shop, a real estate agency, and an editorial studio. Yohei is a creative entrepreneur and author always in search of the next venture.